The Wayward Spirit

A play

Charlotte Hastings

Samuel French — London
New York - Toronto - Hollywood

Rights of Performance by Amateurs are controlled by Samuel French Ltd, 52 Fitzroy Street, London W1P 6JR, and they, or their authorized agents, issue licences to amateurs on payment of a fee. **It is an infringement of the Copyright to give any performance or public reading of the play before the fee has been paid and the licence issued.**

The Royalty Fee indicated below is subject to contract and subject to variation at the sole discretion of Samuel French Ltd.

> Basic fee for each and every
>> performance by amateurs   Code M
>> in the British Isles

The Professional Rights in this play are controlled by Samuel French Ltd.

ISBN 0 573 01938 X

Please see page iv for further copyright information

Printed at Redwood Books, Trowbridge, Wiltshire.

CHARACTERS

George, a male nurse
Captain Anthony Cole
Nurse Rowlands
Sister Winifred, Assistant Matron
Polly, a wardmaid
James Kell FRCS (Sir), consultant surgeon
Father Barrett, hospital chaplain
Chrissy (Christine), Anthony's fiancee
Sister Margaret, Matron
Annie, theatre sister
Brother Francis, a young trainee priest
The Vicar

The scene is St Leofric's (St Leo's) Convent Hospital, East Anglia

Time: the present

SYNOPSIS OF SCENES

ACT I

Scene 1   Anthony's private room

Scene 2   The same. Two weeks later

ACT II

Scene 1   Sister Winifred's office. Two days later

Scene 2   The same. Next day

ACT III

Scene 1   The same. Twelve days later

Scene 2   The same. Six weeks later

In the last scene, the curtain will fall for a few seconds
to denote the passing of eight hours.

Costumes

Sister Winifred's and Sister Margaret's picturesque St. Leo's habits are fully described within the text of the play. They should *on no account* be the usual black habits. The full nuns' costumes, including veils, have been specially made for *The Wayward Spirit* by:

Dauphine's of Bristol
Orchard Road
St George
Bristol
BS5 7HS
Tel: 0117 955 1700 Fax: 0117 940 1220

and may be hired from them, together with all other costumes required for this play.

We show below a sketch drawing of the St. Leo's habit, designed by Charlotte Laurie

Rich purple habit
white lawn veil

C.L.

ACT I

SCENE 1

Captain Anthony Cole's private room in St Leo's Hospital somewhere in Suffolk

A bright summer morning

It is a pleasant light room on hospital plan. The walls are white. There is a casement window in the centre of the back wall, with floor length, dark crimson curtains, giving on to a pleasant view of trees and lawn

There is a door R leading to the main corridor, and a door L leading to the bedroom. Right of the window is a large hospital locker with a tray on it containing bottles and glasses, an enamel hospital bowl, and some folded towels. There is a towel rail on the right of the locker, and on the floor in front of it a large white pile of linen, sheets, towels, and pillow cases. Below the door L is a small wooden armchair and a similar one above the door R. Below the door R is a plain wooden upright chair

On the L wall up stage are two hooks, one holding a man's long warm dressing gown, and on the other a hanger with Anthony's light khaki cardigan jacket. There is also a wall socket for an extension phone. (See plan)

Anthony sits in a light motorised wheelchair RC. He is a pleasant, good-looking man of about thirty, with dark hair and eyes. He is at the moment relaxed and laughing. He is wearing brown cord slacks and a thin lightweight fawn shirt with no tie

George stands on Anthony's right, facing the audience. He is in his forties, a Cockney soul of much humour. He is tall and muscular, as is necessary for his work. He wears the regulation white high-necked uniform tunic and dark trousers. On his right is a small table of the bedside type, set slightly back to allow room to move between it and the chair. On it is a tray with

*a small bowl, a razor case, two small towels, a tin of talcum powder, and
a regimental tie. When the curtain rises, he is just finishing shaving
Anthony*

Nurse Rowlands comes in L, *carrying a large enamel bowl covered with
a white towel. She is a pretty, pleasant girl of about twenty-two in a trim
blue uniform dress and a flowing white cap. Her dress is covered by a
regulation thin white plastic apron. She goes straight across the room and
out* R *without speaking*

George There you are, sir. Smooth as a baby's bottom. (*He puts the razor
on the tray*) And if Miss Chrissy's got any complaints, just refer to me.
(*He picks up a towel and wipes Anthony's face*) Coming as usual, is she?
Two o'clock sharp.

Anthony Two o'clock sharp. For just over a year.

George (*gently*) Been a pretty tough year, hasn't it, sir?

Anthony (*rather grimly*) And I should know.

George You done magnificently, sir. We all think you should have a
medal. (*Suddenly*) Oh, gawd, sir. I forgot to do your back. Better do it
now. Can you lean forward a bit—easy now—that's the ticket.

*Anthony, slightly stiffly, eases himself forward in his chair. George turns
to pick up the dusting powder*

Nurse Rowlands enters R, *carrying the now empty bowl with the towel
crumpled in it and a large black plastic sack labelled "St Leo's
Laundry" in white. She dumps the bag down by the locker and continues
straight across and out* L, *carrying the bowl*

*Anthony's legs suddenly slip. He slides forward helplessly in his chair.
George immediately runs forward*

George Rowley! (*To Anthony*) All right, sir—leave it to us.

Nurse Rowlands runs in L, *to stand on Anthony's left, facing him*

George stands on Anthony's right

You know the drill. Your left under his left…

Nurse Rowlands hooks her arm tightly under Anthony's left armpit. George does the same on the opposite side

Together. Lift...

They lift Anthony a few inches clear of the chair seat and slide him along to sit comfortably back. Then they bend down to straighten his feet and legs against the step of the chair. It is all done quickly and easily with a minimum fuss and effort

Anthony Thank you, Rowley.

Nurse Rowlands gets up and returns to picking up the linen, folding each piece and putting it in the bag

Damn legs. Just wait till I get my crutches. When am I going to get my crutches, George?

Nurse Rowlands' busy hands pause for a fraction of a second in her work

George Get them, sir?
Anthony Yes, George. My crutches. When am I going to get them? Doesn't anybody know?
George Can't say I've heard anything, sir. These things take time.
Anthony Time, yes. But not eternity.
George Well, it will be an eternity if I don't finish you off. Let's get at that back. Can you lean forward again, sir? Like you was before. That's it.

Anthony leans forward. George lifts up the thin shirt, puts talcum powder on his hands, and begins to very gently rub the lower part of Anthony's back

How's that, sir?
Anthony Bliss. Just a bit to the right—that's it.

There is a moment's silence as they work

(*Suddenly*) George, what's it look like?
George Like, sir?

Anthony Yes, my back. To look at? What's it like.

George Well …

Anthony For over a year it's been worked on by one of the finest surgeons in the country, and I've never seen it. Come on George, tell me. What's it like.

George Beautiful, sir. Beautiful.

Anthony Damnit, George. What does it really look like?

George Well, sort of a lunar landscape if you get my meaning. Shadows and hollows—and the stitching, sir. Rows and rows as neat and regular, as if they were ruled. But then, Sir always was a beautiful stitcher. He's noted for it. Sister Annie says when he's retired she's going to give him an embroidery frame.

Anthony Did she indeed. And do we know what he said?

George Oh yes, sir. He said so long as she included a large ball of red silk so he could stitch up her gabby little mouth.

Rowlands They were at it hammer and tongs again this morning, did you hear them?

Anthony The whole place heard them. Sir was early this morning. I saw him and Simmons go by in the Merc. And not ten minutes later they were at each other's throats. Why do they do it? Two brilliant people—he'll never get another theatre sister like her—and they fight like devils. Only in private life. In the theatre they work like angels. I've seen that for myself.

George tucks in Anthony's shirt and eases him gently back into a comfortable sitting position

George Well, I thought he came on a bit strong this morning. Even for him.

Anthony What did he say?

George He said, (*he pauses, laughing*) he said she looked like the other half of a two-headed gargoyle.

Anthony Wow! I hope she had an effective reply.

Rowlands (*dryly*) Very. She threw a scalpel at him.

Anthony Oh no! And?

George He caught it and threw it back at her.

Sister Winifred, Assistant Matron, enters briskly R. She is a tall, slim woman in her early forties. She is dedicated, humane, and full of humour, which doesn't always please her superiors. She wears the St Leo's picturesque habit—a long purple robe, belted at the waist, a broad starched shawl-type collar and a pretty head-dress of white circular lawn raised in front to form a kind of halo effect. She has a beautiful voice. She carries a small kidney bowl containing a ready charged hypodermic syringe and some cotton swabs

Winifred And we are all extremely thankful that they both missed. Good-morning, everybody.

There is a chorus of "Good-morning, Sister Winifred" as she crosses to Anthony's chair

Roll up your sleeve, dear. I've got a little jab for you. (*She puts the bowl on the table*)

Anthony (*rolling up his sleeve*) A jab? Whatever for? I haven't had one of those for a long while, I thought those days were done.

Winifred Just put your arm along the arm of the chair. That's right. Now keep still a second while I find a vein. (*She runs her finger along his arm*) Ah, that will do nicely. (*She swabs his arm with one of the cotton pads, holds the syringe to the light, pushing up the plunger slightly to expel any air bubbles*)

Anthony But what's it *for*?

Winifred You remember Dr O'Connell gave you a check-up last week?

Anthony He didn't seem to find anything sinister.

Winifred Well, he did seem to think you might be just the tiniest bit anaemic. So here's some vitamins. Just in case. Now don't wriggle about —just keep still. Here we go. (*She gives the injection*)

Anthony Ouch! For someone with a vocation, Sister, you pack a right mean needle.

Winifred Good. (*She drops the syringe in the bowl and swabs his arm with another cotton pad*) Now put on a jacket, and a tie. You're having a visitor.

Anthony A visitor? Who?

Winifred Sir.

A flicker of a glance passes slightly between George and Nurse Rowlands

Anthony Sir. This morning?

Winifred (*glancing at her watch*) About half an hour.

Anthony This is a royal visit indeed. And on theatre day, too. I hope he's got permission from Sister Annie. (*He rolls down his sleeve*)

During the following dialogue, George brings Anthony's cardigan from the hanger and helps him into it. George goes back to the table, picks up a regimental tie, gives it to Anthony, then goes back to the table, where he stands cleaning up the razor with a towel. Anthony puts on his tie

Winifred Are you going over to the dining room for lunch, dear?

Anthony No, I've coaxed Sister Appolline into letting me have some sandwiches. I'll go down to the lake till Chrissy comes.

Winifred You like it down there, don't you.

Anthony Yes, it's so peaceful. The birds and the willows. All in the shadow of that great church. Sister, why does a convent have such a large old church instead of the usual small chapel?

Winifred Captain Cole—do you mean to tell me you've been here for a year and never asked how St Leo's came to be formed?

Anthony Well—that year—has been rather busy.

Winifred Of course, my dear. I'm sorry. Well I'm not back on duty for half an hour, so I'll tell you briefly. George knows, of course, but Nurse Rowlands is new to us, so she might like to hear too.

Rowlands I would indeed.

Sister Winifred moves to the window and turns to face the room

Winifred It began at the time when wicked Henry the Eighth was being particularly awful—and turning out all the religious orders—making them redundant. St Leofric's was a monastery then—and their abbot was a Frenchman, Leofric de Croutois. A party of about ten nuns who had had their house burnt came here. They had been wandering in the countryside, living on what they could beg from any charitable villages. They were cold, hungry and exhausted. The brothers took them in, warmed and fed them. But of course, they couldn't remain indefinitely. So Leofric and his flock—with some help from the local people, built them a little house, next to their church—the church you see there now. It's had to be restored, of course.

Rowlands What happened to the Sisters?

Winifred They prospered. They were a nursing order, trained and dedicated. The little house became a hospital and was enlarged. People began to come from afar. Then Leofric returned to France and the monastery fell into disuse and was finally pulled down. But if you go into Sister Freda's little rose garden—it's behind the lecture room—you will see a very old stone. It may even be from the actual building which commemorates the spot. (*She pauses*) But the brothers left us their great church, which you see today. My dears, we are one of the oldest nursing orders in England, and I'm blessed indeed to be part of it.

Rowlands Sister—what a beautiful story.

Anthony Thank you for telling us, I will repeat it to Chrissy when she comes.

There is a knock at the door

Winifred Come in.

Polly enters R, *carrying another of the black laundry bags, but full. She is a thin, wispy little creature who looks considerably younger than her actual eighteen years. She has stooping shoulders and a rather puzzled, somewhat wary little face. She wears a tidy dark blue dress and a flowered pinafore. Her straggly light hair is scraped back into a pigtail in a bright red ribbon*

Polly Please. Miss… Sister…

Anthony Hullo, Polly Flinders—what can we do for you today?

Polly I come for your laundry. (*To Sister Winifred*) Please Miss, Miss Olive says she's got a lot more of the dratted papers and what are you going to do with them—or shall she tell you?

Winifred Oh, goodness—the paperwork. I know very well what I would like to do with it. All right, Polly, you take the bag and get it all down to the laundry. I'll talk to Miss Olive.

Polly Thank you, Miss. (*She indicates the full bag to Nurse Rowlands*) And them's your cleans. (*She goes woefully and slowly to the bags*)

Nurse Rowlands puts in the last pillow case, zips it up and gives it to Polly

(*Mournfully*) Thank you, Nurse.

Anthony What's the matter, Pollyanna? You seem sad this morning.

Polly It's Tuesday, sir.

Anthony What's sad about Tuesday?

Polly It's the day I go out with Bert, sir.

Anthony Then it should be a happy day, shouldn't it?

Polly We don't go out on Tuesdays no more, sir.

Anthony Oh, Polly, why not, what's happened?

Polly (*mournfully*) We go out on Thursday.

Polly gathers up the bag and goes out R, shutting the door behind her

There is a blank pause for a moment, then they are convulsed with laughter

Rowlands Poor little scrap.

Winifred Not at all. She's done wonderfully since she came to us. About five years, isn't it, George?

George Something like that. (*He blows dust off the razor*)

Winifred She was at an orphanage in London. I'd gone there with some supplies they needed. She was like a poor little rabbit—all eyes and teeth and hair. She attached herself to me. When I left, she got out and followed me to the bus stop.

Rowlands Oh, no.

Winifred When I took her back they told me she was a great problem. They were thinking of putting her in a mental home. Well, I thought— you don't put a rabbit in a mental home. So, I phoned Matron and she said bring the little rabbit back with you, Sister, and we'll see what we can do with it.

Anthony And now...

Winifred And now she does a good day's work and she's got a steady boyfriend; so we're all hoping for the best. She isn't really daft, you know. Just a tiny bit muddled now and again.

George She'll be all right with Bert, Sister. He's a bit dim himself at times, but there's no harm in him.

Winifred Well, he's certainly a magnificent gardener. Sister Freda says now he's looking after her roses they practically stand up and sing. (*She picks up her little bowl and crosses R, pausing in the doorway*) Polly will be waiting in my office—she always looks in about this time—for a couple of chocolate biscuits.

She goes out with an airy wave, shutting the door behind her

Rowlands Doesn't she ever stop talking?

Anthony Nope, she's like time's ever rolling stream. But you'd better get used to it. It's her technique.

Rowlands Technique?

Anthony Yes. She rattles on till you gradually find there's a lot of sense somewhere. You either end up laughing or falling asleep, which is probably what she intended. She says sleep and laughter are often more effective than many drugs—and don't cost anything.

George And no forms to fill in either.

Anthony And what's more important, she never brings or forces religion on anyone. On the rare occasions she does, there will be a very good reason.

Rowlands But tell me—is it true she thinks she has a special relationship—with God.

Anthony She probably has.

Rowlands But they say she calls him All-Highest and that he lives in the top left-hand corner of every room she enters. And she talks out loud to him.

George Well, I can't actually say I've seen it for myself. But I reckon everyone is entitled to their own way of thinking and if that's hers I'm all for it.

Rowlands I must say it sounds a bit zany.

Anthony (*sharply*) Nurse Rowlands!

Rowlands (*surprised*) Why, Anthony...

Anthony (*suddenly angry*) Now you listen to me, I'm going to tell you something I'll never forget. So pin your ears back.

George Wait a minute, sir——

Anthony Be quiet. I'm going back in time. It was about six months after I came here. (*He pauses, speaking more quietly*) Sir and I had had a particularly hairy session and when I got back to the ward—do you remember that night, George? The night they couldn't control the pain.

Rowlands Couldn't control—oh, no!

George Now, look, sir——

Anthony Ran out of a certain drug, didn't they, George?

George Sir—it doesn't do to remember——

Anthony Shut up, I said. (*To Nurse Rowlands*) I'll spare you the details. I'll just say that—without exaggeration—I wanted to die.

Rowlands Don't—please don't...

Anthony Why not? You're a nurse, aren't you? Well, then Sister came in. And by that time I'd gone beyond myself. I screamed at her. "Sister,

for God's sake, do something". And did she come in bang on her cue—
about it all being the will of God, and suffering for his death's sake? She
simply took my hand and said "Just keep holding on, Anthony, and we'll
all do the same". And then she went and phoned Sir.

Rowlands Phoned Sir?

Anthony At his house. In London. Didn't she, George?

George Yes, sir. I got the call through for her.

Anthony And he said he'd heard of something. And he rang every
hospital in London—to see if they could help. He could do that you see.
He's that prominent in his profession.

Rowlands But did he get the drug?

Anthony He did. And Simmons came straight down with it—in the
Merc—driving like a maniac. I believe he broke every record on the
A12.

George And you went out like a light for forty-eight hours. And I hope
we never have to go through anything like that again.

Anthony The point is, George, I don't remember the pain; I only
remember how she dealt with it. (*To Nurse Rowlands*) And you
remember that too.

A mellow clock outside chimes the quarter hour

George Gawd—hear that? I'm running out of time. I've got three more
baths to do and I'm helping out with the lunches. Let's get finished—
Rowley, take this will you ? (*He lifts the tray and gives it to Nurse
Rowlands*)

Nurse Rowlands runs to take it off L

George does not pause in his speech

Now let's sort you out, sir. (*He runs the little table over to Anthony and
puts it up in front of his chair*) There you are, sir. Bang to rights. I'll go
over at twelve and collect your sandwiches and a pot of coffee and bring
them over and take you to the lake. I'll fetch you back for two, ready for
Miss Chrissy. Anything else I can do for you before I go?

Anthony No, thank you, George. You've done your usual excellent job.
Off you go, now. Have a good day.

George (*going to the door*) Thank you, sir. And you—(*he pauses for a
second*) you take care.

George goes out R, *shutting the door behind him*

Nurse Rowlands comes running in L

Anthony Rowley—I'm sorry if I was a bit melodramatic just now.
Rowlands That's all right.
Anthony But, I owe a very great deal to Sister Wyn and if you ever again disparage her in my hearing, the first thing I will do when I get my crutches is beat you to death.

Laughing, Nurse Rowlands picks up the full laundry bag and dumps it inside the door L, *talking all the time*

Rowlands That'll be nothing. Sister Carr is probably at this very moment waiting for me with a meat axe.
Anthony (*laughing*) Then fly, sweet angel, fly.

Nurse Rowlands laughs and rushes to the door R

Rowlands Give my love to Chrissy.

She flings the door open just in time to cannon full into Sir as he enters. Sir is a handsome debonair man in his fifties, smart and professional in his long white coat with a stethoscope sticking out of the left-hand pocket

Oh! God.
Sir (*catching her in a firm grip*) What's this—what's this? The Charge of the Light Brigade?
Rowlands Oh! Sir—I beg your pardon—I'm so sorry. Please—I'm in a hurry.
Sir So it appears. But is there not a very rigid rule covering that eventuality—something about the only three accepted reasons which permit running in the corridor.
Rowlands Yes, Sir.
Sir Would you oblige me by repeating them?
Rowlands (*glibly*) One, fire. Two, haemorrhage. Three, childbirth.
Sir Correct. And since, praise God, we are not involved in the third, it will leave you with more thought to apply to the other two.
Rowlands Yes, Sir. Please, Sir—may I go now?

Sir Stand not upon the order, but go quickly.
Rowlands Yes, Sir. Thank you.

She ducks under his arm which is holding the door open, and is heard scurrying away off

Sir shuts the door and comes c *to Anthony's chair, pulling out a cigarette case and lighter. During the next few lines he offers Anthony a cigarette and they both light up*

Sir And now the little darling will rush to join the present vendetta against my poor unfortunate chauffeur.
Anthony Simmons? Why—what's he done.
Sir Apparently—pinching Nurse Potter's bottom.
Anthony Simmy? Never!
Sir Yes, indeed. Nurse Potter spoke to Matron. And Matron spoke to me. Fortunately I was able to reassure her that it would be an isolated incident and I felt sure Nurse Potter's adrenaline had improved as a result.
Anthony So she has survived the ordeal?
Sir Apparently—she broke into verse. "When Simmy's near, protect your rear".

They both laugh. Then Sir, talking all the time, brings an ashtray from the locker to Anthony's chair. Then he turns up to the window and stands looking out

Well, Anthony. I haven't seen you for a day or two. How are you feeling?
Anthony Never better, Sir. The past year gone and Chrissy coming this afternoon. Do you know what has kept me going all this time—apart from my faith in your skill?
Sir Tell me. (*He turns to face Anthony*)
Anthony To walk again—and marry the girl I love. So when do I get my crutches, Sir? Surely you can do something about them.
Sir You're not getting any crutches, Anthony.
Anthony Not getting...
Sir There's been a necessary change of procedure.
Anthony Procedure. Oh! You don't mean more surgery? I don't think—

but of course, if you feel it necessary, I'll go along with whatever you say——

Sir No. No surgery. That's over and done with, for good.

Anthony Well, thank God for that, but——

Sir Listen to me for a moment. Do you remember when you first came to us? From Catterick General?

Anthony Yes. They sent me because you were—are—the finest orthopaedic surgeon in the country.

Sir Well, they sent your X-rays, and when I saw them I said to Annie "Heavens above, who do they think I am—Almighty God?" And Annie said she'd rather like a ruling on that—"So maybe we should start straight away and find out".

Anthony And what have you found out—after a year's work?

Sir That I am very definitely not God.

Anthony As far as I'm concerned, it's a pretty close run thing.

Sir I'm a humble bone surgeon. I can cut and graft and sew. But I can't work miracles.

Anthony You worked one on me.

Sir Let's just say I've been privileged to achieve one thing. I've built you a new spine.

Anthony A new spine!

Sir A new skeletal frame. And we must both thank God. I have. Otherwise you would now be lying flat on your back, staring at the ceiling and hardly able to move at all.

Anthony Which is how I first came to you...

Sir Yes.

Anthony And so—slowly and painfully—you brought me to where I am now. Do you remember saying one day—quite casually—"Now sit up. Anthony. It's high time you sat up". (*He pauses for a second*) And I did. And you laughed and said: "Next stop—the wheelchair." And here I am. Are you going to tell me that's not a miracle? (*He puts out his cigarette*)

Sir Anthony——

Anthony Of course it is. So let's finish it. Get me those crutches and let my feet feel the ground.

Sir I've not been able to do one thing. I've not managed to repair your spinal cord. I thought in the beginning it might be difficult but, I hoped—with the strong frame, rest and drugs—it might improve. But it hasn't worked. That last operation was only partially successful, the remaining damage to the cord is beyond repair.

Anthony Are you—trying to tell me something?

Sir comes slowly forward to the little table. He stubs out his cigarette in the ashtray

Sir (*gently*) You're paraplegic, Anthony. You'll never walk again.

There is a pause

Anthony (*blankly*) Never—walk...

Sir Believe me, I would have done anything rather than have to tell you this.

Anthony I had—to know.

Sir Would you like one of us to speak to Christine for you?

Anthony Chrissy—oh God—she'll have to be told. No, Sir. Thank you— I must do that myself.

Sir Are you sure? I will most willingly do it, or one of the Sisters— particularly Sister Winifred—she could handle such a delicate matter.

Anthony Delicate matter? How do you mean?

Sir I thought you understood. Paraplegic, Anthony. All the functional nerves are gone below the waist.

Anthony So I can never move my legs.

Sir (*gently*) And marriage—the physical side is no longer possible.

Anthony looks at him unbelievingly for a moment. Then he realizes

Anthony (*under his breath*) God Almighty—

Sir crosses to lay a kindly hand on his shoulder

Sir (*gently*) Take it easy—I think it only fair to tell you that I haven't rested entirely on—shall we say—my own lack of laurels.

Anthony What do you mean?

Sir For the past three months there is not a surgeon of any repute whatsoever who has not seen your X-rays and discussed them.

Anthony Sir, I'm not suggesting——

Sir Let me finish. The verdict is unanimous. Last month I spent the weekend with Carr-Sandlesohn—he was my old chief at medical school—and if he can't work miracles—nobody can.

Anthony So, that seems to be that, then?

Sir So, now would you like me to speak to Chrissy?

Anthony (*looking up*) No, you could only tell her the half.

Sir What do you mean—half?

Anthony You can tell her my condition. Only I can tell her I can't marry her.

Sir Now wait. Think. Is that really necessary?

Anthony For God's sake—how could I involve her in such a—an existence?

Sir Don't you think she should have a choice?

Anthony And how would she make such a choice? She'd rush in—full of love—and pity. And then—after—when it came down to the bone—she'd look at me with that pity in her eyes. And it would kill both of us.

Sir Anthony, I beg of you—when you can think straight—don't rush your fences. It's not all gloom and doom——

Anthony It's degradation. And I won't do it.

Sir Now listen to me. You're handicapped—yes, seriously handicapped. But you're neither helpless or hopeless. We will all discuss this and explain to you what can be done. No—don't talk any more for the moment. (*He turns up to the window and back c again*) I'll arrange for you to have a shot just before Chrissy comes. Not immediately—you had one not so long ago.

Anthony A shot? (*He suddenly laughs wryly*) Oh, Sister Wyn's vitamins!

Sir Is that what she said? Well, this will certainly be a bit stronger. And then again this evening—at least we can guarantee you a good night's sleep.

Anthony (*wryly*) Heaviness endureth for the night—but joy cometh in the morning.

Sir No, not joy. Not just yet. But we'll get you sorted—at the moment you're raw. We'll get you rested—and calmer. And then, when you can think straight again, we can talk about rehabilitation.

Anthony Rehabilitation?

Sir Of course. You don't think we're just going to throw you to the wolves, do you?

Anthony But——

Sir Let's leave it for now, Anthony. You're getting exhausted. But let me make a suggestion. With your agreement, I'll come over—let me see—(*he consults his watch*) I've a fair list this afternoon and I've promised Matron I'll do a full ward round later. But I will be free by six. I'll come over and have a word with Chrissy—and if she's too upset to drive back, she can come with us. And Simmy can bring her back later to pick up her car. How do you feel about that?

Anthony (*quietly*) I think, as always, you are kindness and goodness itself.

Sir And when I come over—if you want to scream at me to mind my own business and go away, I promise I will do so without a word. Agreed?

Anthony Agreed.

Sir And don't give way—there is much that—after proper discussion—can be done. Please try to believe that.

His mobile phone beeps. He takes it out of his pocket and switches it on

Kell. ... Oh yes, Annie, I thought it might be you. ... Right, I'm on my way. Which one are we taking first? ... Right. Tell O'Connell he can start the drip. I'll be up in a few seconds. (*He pockets the phone and returns to Anthony*) Goodbye till this evening. I know it sounds impossible—even facetious—but there really is something left. (*He pats Anthony's shoulder and turns to go* R)

Father Barrett enters R, *pausing in the doorway. He is a pleasant man in his early fifties, wearing a cassock and clerical collar. He has a calm gentle face and is a caring and compassionate man*

Barrett Oh! I beg your pardon, Sir.

Sir It's all right, Father. I'm just going. I hope Anthony will be pleased to see you.

Barrett (*very low*) He—knows?

Sir Everything. (*He glances over at Anthony for a second, then says very low*) Be gentle.

Sir goes out, shutting the door

Father Barrett crosses to Anthony

Barrett I've bought you a little drink. (*He puts a small flask on the table in front of Anthony*)

Anthony Thank you. That's kind—later—perhaps.

Barrett I came as soon as we knew Sir would have spoken to you.

Anthony Oh, I see. Everyone has known but me. All waiting for the word—the off—to commiserate.

Barrett (*gently*) Don't take it like that. Everyone here—everyone concerned—is waiting to offer help and support.

Anthony Thank you—but this is something I have to face alone.

Barrett Oh, Anthony—please... (*He brings the upright chair to beside Anthony and sits down*) I beg of you—do not isolate yourself. That is absolutely the wrong attitude to take.

Anthony How can I avoid it? What help is there for me?

Barrett There is plenty of help. My dear boy, this is a terrible—a tragic—thing to happen. But, believe me, it's not the end of the world.

Anthony It's the end of my world. And Chrissy's.

Barrett No, no. There is still plenty left.

Anthony All right. So look at me. Look at me, Father. I'm crippled, incontinent and incapable. If it were you—how would you cope?

Barrett In all honesty, I cannot tell you because I have never been in that situation. But I have known many who have been there and I do feel that if one can retain one's faith—however tenuously, then eventually He will in His love and grace——

Anthony (*suddenly*) Oh, no, Padre. Not that. Soothing words and a little drink—perhaps? But not—please—not the God bit. (*Bitterly*) I reckon that God of yours makes some pretty horrendous mistakes.

Barrett No, Anthony. We make the mistakes, He gets the blame.

Anthony So...

Barrett (*gently*) So look back on the past year. The stress, the pain and the courage with which you faced it. He gave you that courage, Anthony. He brought you through. He never once let you down.

Anthony Well, he has now!

Barrett No—for the moment it feels like it. But with His help and understanding...

Anthony (*bitterly*) What will He do now? Fly through that window on a cloud—shouting "Take up thy bed and walk"?

Barrett When you have got over the first shock—and talked to Chrissy——

Anthony To tell her I can't marry her?

Barrett Anthony, *no*!

Anthony Don't sound so horrified. Don't you realize that in the circumstances it's the only right thing to do?

Barrett No, it's *not* right. There are many instances—in similar circumstances—which with knowledge and goodwill—and love—have resulted in a compassionate loving—and happy partnership.

Anthony Well, I won't insult her by offering that. There's the sex problem as well. Or perhaps that's something you don't understand.

Barrett Understand? Why not? (*Quietly*) We do take a vow of celibacy, remember.

Anthony That's a bit different, isn't it? You have a choice.

Barrett Perhaps that choice makes it harder.

Anthony (*suddenly*) I'm sorry, Padre. I know you have to do your job— and in accordance with your beliefs—but I'm tired—could you, please, just go.

Barrett If that is what you want. But remember, you are surrounded by love and every desire to help. And, above all—I beg you—don't break Chrissy's heart. If there has to be a decision, let it be hers.

Anthony (*suddenly breaking*) For God's sake—will you *get out*? (*He beats violently on the table*)

Father Barrett gets up. He puts a gentle hand on Anthony's violent ones and stops them

Barrett If you wish me to go, then I will do so. (*He takes the upright chair back and turns*) But if—later—you feel you need me—or anyone else—you have only to send word.

Father Barrett goes out R, *closing the door behind him*

Anthony sits very still for a second. Then he reaches for the flask, looks at it for a moment, and suddenly thrusts it into his jacket pocket. He sits still for a second, then suddenly propels his chair away from the table, pushing it aside. He swings his chair round so that it is up R, *half facing the door* R. *He places his hands firmly on the arms, braces himself and begins a frantic and pitiful struggle to stand. Each time he manages to raise himself a few inches, his useless legs give way and he falls back in the chair. He does this three times. Then, suddenly, he goes into shock, panting for breath; he seizes first one and then the other of his legs under the knee, bending and twisting it. Then he beats frantically at them—all to no avail*

Anthony (*suddenly shouting*) No! (*He drags the flask from his pocket, unscrews it and drains it. Then he hurls it* R *to shatter against the door. He falls forward with his arms on his knees and his head bent on to them—struggling with harsh uncontrollable sobs*)

Chrissy (*calling off* R) Anthony—Anthony!

Chrissy runs in R. *She is in her early twenties, flushed and pretty in a light summer dress. She carries two filled carrier bags, one with a bottle sticking out, and a large bunch of flowers*

(*She pauses in the doorway*) Anthony—I've got the whole day—a whole wonderful day! (*She starts to run towards him*)

He raises his head and screams at her

Anthony Go away! For God's sake—don't touch me! *Go away!*

She stops dead, the parcels and flowers falling from her hands

CURTAIN

SCENE 2

Two weeks later

Anthony's room. The only furniture change is that the little table is now against R *wall above the door*

Anthony is sitting in his chair RC, *half back to the main door. Chrissy has brought the small armchair from* L *and is sitting facing him a few feet away. She is wiping her eyes*

Anthony Oh, for God's sake, Chrissy—stop crying. It doesn't help anything.
Chrissy So what am I supposed to do? Race along the corridors waving a balloon?
Anthony That isn't funny.
Chrissy Nothing's funny any more. It's two weeks now since—we knew. And all we've done is sit and tear each other to pieces.
Anthony I know. I'm sorry——
Chrissy I still don't understand. I've told you over and over again—I love you and I'll stand by you. So why are you so—so adamant—that you won't marry me?
Anthony Because I won't offer you a marriage that would be a degradation and a sham—

Chrissy It doesn't have to be either.

Anthony Doesn't it? All right, I'll tell you again. So try and take it in.

Chrissy But——

Anthony Just listen, will you. So we get married, I love you, and I'll want you—I'll want you like hell. And there's absolutely nothing I can do about it.

Chrissy So we can't have the icing. Do we have to throw out the cake?

Anthony A pretty unpalatable cake.

Chrissy Is that the only way you want me—in bed?

Anthony (*angrily*) In all our five years together have I ever—at any time—given you cause to think that?

Chrissy No. Perhaps—as it happens—it might have been better if you had. At least we'd have had something...

Anthony Stop it. I never knew you could be so tough.

Chrissy Maybe you're not the only one who's had a tough year—Now you're...

Anthony I'm sorry—but I know it would be too much for both of us. And for your sake I won't take the risk.

Chrissy I will.

Anthony Because at this moment, you're filled with a holy glow of self sacrifice. You see yourself in a spotless overall and your arms full of flowers.

Chrissy What's wrong about that?

Anthony You won't face the reality. The apron won't stay spotless. And what you're carrying could be something very different from a bunch of flowers.

Chrissy And you're all puffed up with a burning sense of righteousness. Next you'll be telling me you're going to cut me right out of your life.

Anthony (*quietly*) I've already done it.

Chrissy gets up

Chrissy Anthony—what do you mean?

Anthony The papers came through yesterday. All the preliminary arrangements are made.

Chrissy What are you talking about? What arrangements?

Anthony I've applied for a place at Wellington Court.

Chrissy Why haven't you told me about this? And what the hell is Wellington Court.

Anthony It's a high class nursing home—for disabled army officers. In Surrey.

Chrissy Anthony, no!

Anthony (*steadily*) Fully trained nursing staff round the clock. And facilities for some kind of social life. Outings and I believe there's a billiards room. And a library. One learns to work—with one's hands—bits of carpentry—and things. (*He falters, but makes himself continue*) It'll all help—to—pass the time.

Chrissy For God's sake—haven't these past five years meant anything—anything at all—to you?

Anthony I do know it sounds cold-blooded—but it really is best. A quick clean break.

Chrissy And while you're merrily messing about with your cold-blooded bits of fretwork—what is supposed to happen to me?

Anthony Chrissy, darling—you're young—and pretty—and eminently desirable—you'll soon forget me—and marry somebody else.

Chrissy Oh yes. On the rebound. And suppose I don't happen to love this somebody else?

Anthony At least he will be able to prove that he loves you.

Chrissy (*suddenly flaring up*) That's a damnable thing to say.

Anthony It's a damnable situation.

Chrissy I keep on telling you. It doesn't have to be like this.

Anthony No! But we have to be practical. I'll not let you down, Chrissy.

Chrissy Nor I you.

Anthony Apparently I'm getting a generous pension. (*Quietly*) I'm arranging to make over a third to you.

Chrissy (*aghast*) Anthony!

Anthony We've been together five years. It's the least I can do.

Chrissy (*blazing*) You know what you're doing? You're—you're buying me off.

Anthony Please... Please don't look at it like that...

Chrissy There's no other way to see it. Oh, Anthony—how could you?

Anthony Chrissy—stop—please. It's pointless to go on arguing like this——

Chrissy I've told you how I feel. You seemed determined not to give me a chance.

Anthony You'd never cope.

Chrissy How do you know?

Anthony You don't realize. Sometimes I think you don't even listen.

Chrissy So I'm listening now.

Anthony Apart from—other things—I'm going to need round the clock
  nursing procedures for the rest of my life.

Chrissy We'll have help from the district nurses.

Anthony They won't be there all the time. The bulk of it will fall on you.

Chrissy So—I'll cope. If you'll come off your high horse and let me.

Anthony You see—I can't make you understand.

Chrissy So explain. (*Angrily*) Explain. Go on.

Anthony Don't make me——

Chrissy I'm listening!

Anthony All right—here's an example. You'll come home one evening,
  probably after a hard day, you'll be hot and tired and you'll want a warm
  bath and a double gin and—let's face it—a bit of a cuddle——

Chrissy So?

Anthony (*shouting*) The first thing you'll probably have to do is to wade
  straight in—and clean me up!

Chrissy (*shouting back*) So, I'll drink the gin first!

Anthony (*topping her*) And I hope it chokes you! (*He swings his chair
  violently over to the window and sits with his back to the room*)

*Chrissy drops into the chair with her arm along the back and breaks into
bitter sobs*

Sister Winifred enters R

Winifred I could hear you right along the corridor—why, what's this?
  Oh! Chrissy, my dear—don't... (*She drops on her knees beside Chrissy
  and pulls out a handkerchief*) Here—wipe your eyes. And stop crying.
  (*She wipes Chrissy's eyes*)

Chrissy still sobs

  Now take a deep breath—no—come along—another. Now blow your
  nose——

Chrissy does so

  That's it, and again—a good hard one. There that's better. (*She gives her
  the handkerchief*) No—keep it. From what appears to be happening
  you'll need it again. (*She gets up and crosses to Anthony's chair*)

Chrissy is left sniffing and dabbing her eyes

Sister Winifred stands beside Anthony's chair and speaks very firmly

And since you appear to be the only person here to cause such distress, I think some sort of apology might be called for.

Anthony (*sullenly*) She asked for it.

Winifred Anthony, you will go straight over and apologise to Chrissy—at once.

Anthony (*still sullen*) You—can't make me.

Sister Winifred takes his chair, turns it round and pushes it across in front of Chrissy

Winifred Do it. (*She crosses over to the window and stands with her back to the room, looking out*)

There is a pause

(*Without turning*) I'm waiting.

Anthony (*stiffly*) Chrissy. Sister thinks I should make you an apology. In accordance with her instructions I now formally do so. (*He swings his chair round and moves angily away* RC *with his back to her*)

Winifred (*turning back*) That is the most outrageous behaviour I have ever witnessed. (*She comes down to him*) Anthony Cole, you know what's the matter with you—you're spoilt.

Anthony (*swinging round again to face her*) Spoilt.

Winifred Yes. Completely and utterly spoilt. We've nursed you and admired your courage for the past year, and now—when the real crunch comes, what do you do?

Anthony I get angry.

Winifred Yes. And that's a natural reaction, to be accepted. But you're turning that anger on everyone else. Lashing out and determined to hurt all those you love and who love you.

Anthony I want to hurt the whole bloody world!

Winifred And destroy your life completely. And Chrissy's, too.

Anthony I——

Winifred Now, you be quiet and listen to me. We've had a long committee meeting about you, and I've been given the job—which is apparently going to be a thankless one—of telling you our findings.

Anthony What findings?

Winifred The best arrangements for your future.

Chrissy Oh, he's too proud to listen to your arrangements. He's already made his own.

Winifred His own? What do you mean?

Chrissy He's going into some very grand nursing home. For officers—somewhere in the country. It's called Wellington Court.

Winifred Anthony—no! Couldn't you have waited and discussed it with us?

Anthony I can't stay here indefinitely. You're not a convalescent home.

Winifred No, but when something like this happens to our people, we don't just throw them out. Really, Anthony, this is very inconsiderate of you.

Anthony I've got to stand on my own two feet... (*He breaks off, laughing harshly*) Oh, God did you hear that. Stand on my own two feet. What a sick joke. Laugh of the year.

Winifred Stop tormenting yourself. And you can just put those plans for Wellington Court on hold, while we discuss the plans we've made for you.

Anthony Plans for what?

Winifred Rehabilitation.

Anthony There's nothing to rehabilitate.

Winifred Just wait and see. Now—(*She brings the upright chair* C *and sits down between them*) I think Sir has already said. You may be handicapped but you're not helpless. Thanks to him you have a strong spine and your arms are strong also—which means you have good control over your torso. So it's really only your legs.

Anthony Only...

Winifred So we have to compensate for them.

Anthony How?

Winifred I'm coming to that in a minute. Because that's where we really have had an amazing piece of luck.

Anthony *Luck?*

Winifred I had a long and very interesting talk with your commanding officer.

Anthony You what?

Winifred Sir got on to the M.o.D. about you. You'll get the forms later. Well, there was a query and they rang back. But Sir wasn't available, so Olive put him through to me. A most charming and delightful man, Colonel Piggot-Jones.

Anthony Sister—you don't mean—you actually talked to Porker-Jones.

Winifred No, dear—his name's Piggot—Oh! I see. You can't—you can't—seriously—call him—Porker...

Anthony Only when we're being polite.

Winifred But that's quite disgraceful. Such a polite and kindly man——

Anthony My dear Sister Winifred, on a good day Porker-Jones can slice through a man's backside with half a dozen words at twenty paces.

Winifred Well, I was more than twenty paces away on the telephone, so my backside is still attached.

In spite of themselves, both Anthony and Chrissy laugh

Anthony I really can't believe you.

Winifred Do you know he breeds canaries?

Anthony (*in a falsetto squeak*) Canaries!

Winifred Yes. Actually I think his wife does most of the work. But he is apparently very knowledgeable about breeding. Do you know, he told me that in the mating season—(*she breaks off*)—well perhaps not. And he said some very pleasant things about you.

Anthony Did he indeed?

Winifred He said you were a very promising and ambitious young officer—and he was very sorry about it all—and that they would look after you. He personally sent his warm wishes and regards. And all the boys sent their best and were—were—rooting—is that right—rooting?

Anthony That's right.

Winifred Rooting for you. And they were making his life a misery because they were collecting for a wedding present and wanted to find out what to do. (*Triumphantly*) So then I told him about the chair.

Anthony *Chair?*

Winifred Well, to start with, you're getting this wonderful chair—it's only just on the market, and if the brochure is to be believed—and it should be unless this awful Government has suddenly cancelled the Trade Descriptions Act—it's really amazing.

Anthony Amazing. How?

Winifred It's not motorised like that one. It runs on little batteries. But you can get them quite easily by post—of course those wretched forms have to filled in.

Anthony So the forms are filled in, what does it do?

Winifred It gives you your freedom.

Anthony My freedom—it only pushes me along.

Winifred Apparently it does everything but fly. And since you're Army, not Air Force, that needn't worry you.

Anthony So I'm sitting in this atomic marvel. What happens then?

Winifred You can go anywhere. Parks and gardens, streets. All the streets, Anthony. Shops, supermarkets, and theatres and cinemas—a lot of them have facilities for chairs. And museums and libraries. Opportunities for study and research—you might even get a little job. Can't you see, Anthony—so many things opening all the time.

Anthony But——

Winifred And indoors—you can go into the kitchen, and wash up and cook. Helping Chrissy with the chores. Anthony, there is absolutely no need ever just to sit and look at the wall.

Anthony Sister, hold on a moment.

Winifred No—because now we come to the hoist.

Anthony Hoist?

Winifred Yes. We don't have them here because the beds have pulleys. You'll have to get that for yourself. But we can put you in touch with one of the disabled organisations.

Chrissy So tell us about the hoist.

Winifred It's quite simple. Electric, of course. A harness which lifts and swings you from one place to another. Your bed to your chair and back again. And it can be used in the bathroom. You'll learn as you go. Oh, yes! And there's Chrissy's car.

Chrissy What about the car?

Winifred Fortunately it's an estate. So Simmons is going to fix a ramp at the back. You press a button and the doors open, then another button and the ramp comes down—so you just drive in—and away you go. Now, honestly, can we do more?

Anthony You've forgotten the most important thing—the nursing procedure.

Winifred No, we haven't. We know this was very much at the heart of the matter for you. So that's where Chrissy comes in.

Anthony She does *not*! Once and for all—she does not!

Chrissy Anthony, listen——

Anthony I will not have her involved. She doesn't understand what is entailed.

Winifred She will when she's trained.

Anthony What the hell do you mean—trained?

Winifred We've offered her two weeks training—more, if she wishes—
here at St Leo's.

Anthony You've what?

Winifred It'll all work out well. She says she can get the time off, and she
can stay here, in the nurses' home. And most of the time she'll be with
you. But every morning she'll come on duty in the ward with the rest of
us, just as if she were one of the team. She'll learn exactly what it all
entails and how to cope in an efficient and natural way. And since you
yourself will be one of that team—in time—so will you.

Anthony Never! (*He swings his chair round with his back to them*)

Winifred Then you're a very proud and ungrateful young man and you
don't deserve the time and trouble that's been wasted trying to help you
both. Quite apart from the fact that you seem determined to break her
heart.

Chrissy Please don't say that.

Winifred Well, I don't see what more I can do. I'll try not to persuade you
any further, Anthony. If you're determined to stand on your pride——

Anthony It's all I've got left.

Winifred And you'll find it a very sterile thing. So we shall have to let
you go.

Chrissy You can't send him away...

Winifred We have already agreed we are not a convalescent home. You
may make your arrangements to go to Wellington Court as soon as you
wish. (*She gets up with an air of finality, returns the chair to its place
and goes back to Chrissy*)

Chrissy But he can't...

Winifred He can. But I have one last thing to say to you, Anthony. Will
you listen? Because I shan't say it again.

He does not answer

Chrissy Anthony, please——
Anthony Go on.

*Sister Winifred makes the next speech very quietly, without emotion—but
she is very determined indeed*

Winifred You are not a sick man. You are strong. And you are young. You
have many more years to live. Go to your chosen place. You will be well
cared for. You will be warm and clean and fed—and they will try and

stimulate your mind. But you will be among people like yourself—and some worse—who perhaps have given up. And as the years go on, you will become older and more isolated. You will be alone. And, there may come a time when you begin to think—did you perhaps condemn Chrissy to this same half life.

Chrissy Oh, don't—don't. You're trying to break him down.

Winifred (*relentlessly*) *You*—have to make the decision, Anthony. The cold hard prop of your stony pride—or the warm and loving heart?

Anthony suddenly bows his head into his hands

Chrissy How can you be so cruel? (*She makes an involuntary move towards him*)

Sister Winifred lays a gentle but firm hand on her arm to check her

Winifred (*very quietly*) No, Chrissy. He must come to you.

There is a pause. Anthony sits very still, fighting the last bitter battle against his pride. Then, very slowly, he lowers his hands and propels his chair towards Chrissy. She goes towards him, meeting him C, *with Sister Winifred standing immediately behind them*

Anthony Chrissy...

He holds out his hand to her; she takes it. Sister Winifred turns and goes to the window, with her back to them

I tried—to be strong. I thought I was right. Now—I'm not sure. I don't know—what to do. (*He leans against her exhausted*) Chrissy—please help me. Suddenly-I'm so tired.

Chrissy kneels down beside him, holding him close, cradling his head in her arms. Pause. Sister Winifred turns to look at them. She smiles. Then, without speaking, she looks across at the left-hand corner and nods. She crosses UC *behind them to the door* R *and opens it. Anthony and Chrissy look up*

Sister...

Sister Winifred turns with her hand on the door knob

Please don't go—— (*He holds out his hand*)

She crosses down to them

This is the second time since I came here that you brought me back from the brink. How can I ever thank you?

Winifred By accepting the fact that you still have a life together.

Chrissy Oh, we'll try——

Father Barrett enters briskly R, carrying a folded newspaper and some envelopes

Barrett Good-morning. Anthony. I've brought you papers and the post. (*He pauses*) Now—what's this? Something tells me I've come at rather tense moment.

Winifred Never were you more welcome. Oh, Father—it is all settled. They have agreed.

Barrett Agreed?

Winifred To all the arrangements. And they are to be married.

Barrett Oh, well done, well done. How splendid. (*He takes Anthony's hand*) My dear boy—congratulations. And Chrissy, my dear—(*he takes her hand too*) I wish you both so well. God bless and be with you on this day.

Anthony And you must both come to our wedding. How could we get married without you—who made it possible. (*He pauses very briefly*) You will come—you must. Say you will come.

Winifred (*quietly*) We shall have to see.

Anthony Have to see? Why? Surely there is no reason—you can't mean you're not allowed to come?

Winifred Just wait a little, Anthony.

Anthony No. If you can't come to us—we'll—we'll stay with you. Chrissy, I've got the most wonderful idea. Why don't we get married here—at St Leo's—where we've been given so much help—and so much love.

Chrissy We have no family to consider.

Winifred So—(*working it all out*) for that day you'll belong to us. I'll ask Sir to give Chrissy away. I'm sure he would.

Chrissy And Sister Annie for my bridesmaid. We must do it, Sister—we must.

Anthony How do we get it arranged? Who do I have to ask—can you let me know? It will be the most wonderful thing—we will never forget it.

Chrissy It will be the cement which holds us together!

They pause looking at Sister Winifred, then Father Barrett

Please tell us how it can be arranged.

Barrett (*quietly*) My dears—my dear children. I'm so sorry…

Chrissy Sorry?

Barrett You cannot be married in St Leo's. (*He pauses for a second*) You are not Catholics.

CURTAIN

ACT II

Scene 1

Sister Winifred's office

A pleasant room on the same hospital plan as the previous Act. The same white walls, large centre window and long dark crimson curtains. The same doors, R to the main corridor, L to the bedroom

R of the window, against the back wall, is a large modern metal filing cabinet. L of the window, against the back wall, is a bookcase, crammed with books. Up L above the bedroom door, a small table—the one from Act I will do. On it is a large wicker filing basket stacked with papers. (Right at the bottom must be a file with a glossy dark blue cover)

L below the bedroom door is a small armchair and on the wall above it, a large framed colour reproduction of The Last Supper

Above the main door R is a small armchair and below it a small upright chair. Above this chair hangs a large crucifix

Centre, slightly angled R to face the main door is Sister Winifred's big oak kneehole desk, with a comfortable swivel chair behind it. On the tidy desk is a pentray, a very large note pad and a telephone. In the middle drawer of the desk is a large envelope (for the blue file), a green covered file of papers clipped in (Nurse Rowlands), and a bunch of keys. Everything is meticulously neat and organised

When the Curtain *rises, the phone is ringing furiously. Then it stops for a couple of seconds and begins to ring again*

Sister Winifred enters hurriedly R, carrying more books and papers. She has come straight from the ward and wears a big starched apron over her purple habit

Winifred All right—I'm coming! (*She goes to the desk, puts down the papers and files and picks up the phone*) Sister Winifred... Oh, Olive dear—I am so sorry—I've only just come off the ward. What can I do for you? ... The paperwork? Oh, yes—I do know. Drowning in a sea of wood pulp. Was there anything in particular? ... Last month's drug list? I am so sorry—I know I have it somewhere. ... Of course I'll look for it. Right now—hold on. (*She starts to put down the phone then stops*) Could you just remind me what it looks like? ... A glossy dark blue folder with a gold crown on the cover—Department of Medicine—oh, I know. Hold on. (*She puts down the phone and crosses to the small table with the large basket on it, starts to look through papers, then exclaims impatiently and takes the basket to the desk. She turns it upside down, gives it a smart slap, and lifts it off the contents—on the top is a glossy dark blue folder. She picks up the phone*) I've found it. Page four—yes. ... (*She turns the pages*) Number? RBL—yes, here we are—RBL. RBL. 7941GK. Anything else? ... I sign on the last page? Under what? Authorised Personnel? Good gracious—how important that sounds. Yes—and we're not nursing. We're just filling in forms. I'll get it to you as soon as possible and I really do think we must write a stiff letter to that tiresome little man. The one in Downing Street, dear. ... You don't think he can read? Well, we'll have to go through all three hundred and sixty of them until we find one who can. (*She puts down the phone, picks up a pen and signs the file, then finds a large envelope in her desk drawer, seals up the file, puts it back in the desk drawer and closes it. She crosses* L, *takes off her apron and hangs it on a peg. She returns to her desk and sits in the swivel chair*)

There is a knock at the door

(*She straightens up, calling rather wearily*) Come in.

Sister Margaret, the Matron, enters R. *She is between forty-five and fifty, tall and distinguished in her purple habit and white veil. She is firm and authoritative and has a pleasant, level voice*

Matron Good-morning, Sister. Can you spare me a few moments? As you are so busy, I thought I would come to you, rather than ask you to come to me. Father Barrett will be joining us in a few minutes.
Winifred Thank you, Matron. Please sit down. (*She gets up, indicating the swivel chair*)

Matron sits down. Sister Winifred fetches the small upright chair and sits down opposite Matron

Matron We will not keep you long. I believe you have had rather a busy morning.

Winifred Yes indeed. But I am now free until midday.

Matron How is Captain Cole this morning?

Winifred I haven't seen him myself, but Sister Carr did the morning visit and she reported that he is greatly improved in spirit. And Chrissy too.

Matron The matter has been splendidly resolved—and we all know who we have to thank for it.

Winifred I usually find that the Almighty in His own time and His own way decides what is best for all of us.

Matron Has Father Barrett spoken to you?

Winifred No, not again. He had already made it quite plain there was no more to discuss. (*Suddenly*) Matron—is there really no more—even to discuss—about the wedding.

Matron Sister, we have to accept that. If we had a private chapel, but in our church it is totally unacceptable. Unless, of course, one of them were a Catholic. Believe me, Sister Winifred, I regret this as much as you do—but it isn't just our own view. It is also a matter of civil law under the registrar.

Winifred I know, I know. But they are so disappointed. Anthony has gone through so much—(*suddenly*) Matron—it isn't fair.

Matron Now please, Sister. You must not allow yourself to become emotional.

Winifred I can't help it.

Matron Listen to me, Sister. Are you not dangerously near breaking one of our most important rules? And forming a personal relationship...

Winifred Perhaps—I am.

Matron Then you must be strong. Remember—and accept—your only personal relationship—may be with God.

Winifred Matron, how can I help it. I have nursed that boy day and night for a year. I have watched his pain—and the courage with which he faced it. How can I not feel personally involved?

Matron You must fight against it. Fortunately they will soon be gone from here. Remember only that you were able to help them—and I assure you that eventually you will find peace.

Winifred But is it really so much to ask? Is there really no way at all that we might get permission. Of course it would have to be right from the top—(*she pauses*) the very highest source——

Matron Sister Winifred—I beg you to put out of your mind any idea of a return ticket to Rome.

Winifred It is said—that the Holy Father is a very compassionate man...

Matron Didn't you hear what I just said? It's not a matter of compassion, it's a matter of law.

Winifred Someone—somewhere—must be able to overturn an unfair law——

Matron Now you have gone too far. Use your common sense. And you know we are trying to compensate. We do not yet know if they will be married in the village. But we will be giving them a little wedding lunch in the big hall. Sister Appolline is already happily planning the menu— and I am told on very good authority that she has quite fantastic ideas about a wedding cake. Everyone will want to be there.

Winifred It is rather a sad thought that all this has arisen through an original gesture of great compassion in the middle ages.

Matron How do you mean?

Winifred The brothers gave us our church. If we had built our own chapel—it would have been an open one for all denominations—class, race or creed. (*Suddenly*) Oh dear—I do so wish people would just take the time and trouble to think ahead.

Matron (*laughing*) Five hundred years? Can you honestly say yourself that you ever have the time to look ahead for five minutes.

Winifred Five seconds more like.

Matron Exactly. And speaking of time—where has Father Barrett got to? May I just phone—thank you. (*She pulls the phone towards her and dials three digits*) Still engaged—well, well... (*She replaces the phone and dials three digits*) Hullo—can you tell me if Father Barrett's phone is out of order? He seems to have been engaged all morning. ... Since ten o'clock? Well, what on earth... Matron here. Do you know who he might be talking to? ... He got the number himself. I see. Thank you. (*She replaces the phone*) It must be some kind of emergency. But he very definitely said he wanted to see us together—so it must be something special—we should wait a little longer. (*She smiles*) Dear Father Barrett—do you know what he calls you?

Winifred At times I can imagine.

Matron "The Wayward Spirit".

Winifred Wayward?

Matron It's from a short poem. I can't remember the author—though Father Barrett told me at the time. "The wayward spirit that turns against the wind".

Winifred That's a very kind and poetic way of calling me a confounded nuisance. Am I a confounded nuisance, Matron?

Matron Sometimes. How long have we been working together?

Winifred Fifteen years. I was here for five years before you.

Matron Ah, yes. My predecessor was Sister Mathilde. I remember her vividly. Very slight, tense, dark—with somewhat strange eyes. One could always see her as in the last stages of burning at the stake.

Winifred That has always filled me with horror. To be going there because of one's faith. Thinking—all the way—I have given you my trust, my life—you cannot let this happen. And when it did, in the last few agonised seconds, to know it was all for nothing. That must be the final spark of utter disillusionment.

Matron Would you have died in disillusionment?

Winifred No! In anger. Great burning anger—hotter than the fire itself.

Matron Oh, Sister Winifred—you do say the most *uncomfortable* things.

Winifred Is that it then—always the uncomfortable things—always against the wind?

Matron I have learned to live with it. We must not be sentimental, Sister. But you are the heart which binds St Leo's together—I have the utmost trust and respect both in you and for you. I hope that as long as we are privileged to work together we will be friends.

Winifred Thank you. (*She smiles*) And I will try and watch the way the wind is blowing.

There is a knock at the door

(*Slightly irritated*) Oh, bother. (*Calling*) Come in.

Polly enters R, *carrying a large pile of files in assorted covers*

Polly Good-morning, Miss. (*She makes a sort of little bob at Matron*) Good-morning, ma'am.

Matron Good-morning.

Winifred Oh, Polly not now—perhaps later.

Polly Please Miss—it has to be now. (*She holds out the files*) Miss Olive sent you these—(*she hands over the files*) and she says if you don't know what to do with them, ring her and she'll tell you about her new idea...

Sister Winifred takes the files, puts them on top of the basket on the little table, and returns to the desk

Winifred Thank you, Polly.
Polly And she wants them back by six o'clock tomorrow. (*She pauses, puzzled*) Now what was it—oh yes, I remember. (*Triumphantly*) Or else! (*She turns to go* R)
Winifred Thank you. Oh, Polly. Just a moment—you've forgotten your chocolate biscuits—and now, come to think of it, you haven't had them for nearly a week.
Polly Thank you, Miss. But I won't be having them no more.
Winifred But why? I thought you enjoyed that last little nibble in bed?
Polly It's Bert, Miss. He don't like crumbs in the sheets.

She drifts out R

Matron and Sister Winifred look at each other for a moment

Winifred So now we know.
Matron We shall have to do something about it. The question is what and how? (*Slowly*) This is going to be a tricky one, Sister, it's an ethical issue.
Winifred I know. But I think in this case it can be justified.
Matron How are we going to explain to her?

Sister Winifred suddenly snaps her fingers

Winifred (*triumphantly*) We explain to Bert.
Matron Oh, what a splendid idea. (*She pauses*) That's just a little bit—tricky, too. (*Firmly*) Well, if it has to be done, I'll do it.
Winifred But—I——
Matron Sister Winifred, just for once, will you recognize that there are occasionally things you can't do yourself?
Winifred Of course—I'm sorry, Matron.
Matron I confess it may be rather embarrassing. After all—it is man's talk. (*Suddenly*) But of course—Father Barrett—I'll ask him.

Winifred No, Matron. Not poor Father Barrett. George!
Matron George?
Winifred Yes, good old honest George. He is a trained nurse—and he is not bound by our rules. It's the perfect solution. Whyever didn't I think of it straight away?
Matron Sister Winifred, what should I do without you? (*Suddenly serious*) We should have anticipated this before.
Winifred Yes—we should. But time slips by so quickly.

Suddenly Matron begins to laugh

Matron Oh, Sister Winifred, dear Sister Winifred—the little rabbit has suddenly grown up and kicked us in the teeth.

They both break into relieved laughter. There is a sudden burst of noise and running of feet off stage R

Annie (*off*) And get out from under my feet!

There is a brief knock at the door, which is then flung open to admit Annie herself. She is a small person in her late twenties, but with tremendous force of character. She would be good looking if she relaxed, which she never does. She is not a nun, but a nursing Sister, and wears a dark blue dress, white crossover apron, and a neat white cap on her red hair. She is waving a large piece of printed paper

What the hell is the meaning of this?
Matron Calm down, Sister Annie, calm down.
Annie Calm down-calm down! This is a disaster—it's more—it's an insult.
Winifred Well, if it's anything to do with that paper, stop waving it and give it to me—and then perhaps we can sort things out.
Annie You'd ruddy well better—and to make things worse, you've actually signed it. You must be out of your mind.
Winifred We'll decide that when I've read it. Now, perhaps you will take a couple of deep breaths and sit down, Sister Annie.

Annie puts the piece of paper in Sister Winifred's hand. Matron gets up and takes Annie's arm

Matron Come and sit down.

She takes Annie to the small armchair L and sits her down, remaining on her right

Winifred This appears to be the monthly drug list for the theatre. It would be checked and authenticated by both the dispensary and the secretary, before I signed it.

Annie Then you're all half-wits.

Winifred So I signed it, what is wrong?

Annie Look at the heading "antibiotics".

Winifred I'm looking.

Annie So it's half what it was last month. What are you going to do about that? Huh? (*Louder*) What are you going to do about that?

Winifred Neither the dispensary nor the secretary usually make mistakes, especially about drugs.

Annie Well, they've made a complete cock-up this time. (*Furiously*) And what am I supposed to use for antibiotic? Washing-up water?

Winifred If there is a mistake, Annie, you can be sure it will be put right. (*She puts the paper in the middle desk drawer*)

Annie It had better be. And double quick or else.

Sir enters. He has changed back into an immaculate dark suit. He closes the door behind him

Sir Excuse me, ladies. But do I hear the dulcet tones of a little ginger haired she-cat who has the temerity to call herself my assistant in certain matters of anatomical repair?

Annie You keep out of it.

Sir My sweet soul—there is nothing I would actually like better—but you really do loom too large on my horizon.

Annie (*between her teeth*) G-r-r-r-r-r.

Matron (*suddenly*) Stop it, both of you. (*She moves up to the windows and turns to face them*) I regret to say this, but, really, you both behave like two ill-mannered children. I appreciate you are often overworked and are overtired, but just for the immediate time I must ask you both to calm down, and perhaps a small apology might not be out of place.

Annie So who apologises to whom?

Matron It is distasteful for me to tell one of the most distinguished surgeons in England—but he should be aware he also has one of the most skilful and experienced theatre sisters in the business.

Sir Oh, she knows a hawk from a handsaw if that's what you mean.

Matron She is your right hand and left hand and probably both your feet as well. Need I say more?

Sir Matron, I was once told that when Matron reprimands anyone, she can remove three layers of skin. You have taken two. I stand before you flayed and penitent and abjectly abase myself before you both.

Annie Abase? Don't make me laugh!

Sir I will now proceed to kneel.

Annie Don't you ruddy well dare!

Sir But I have——

Annie James Kell—the day you kneel before me, I will personally strangle you with the thickest and strongest length of catgut I can find in the theatre!

Sir That's my girl! Matron, will you now agree I have been reprieved?

Matron (*laughing*) Oh, get along with you both.

Sir (*smiling gently at Annie*) Scalpel slinger!

Annie Bone basher!

There is a knock at the door

Winifred Oh, dear—everybody but the Queen! (*She opens the door*)

Chrissy is outside with Anthony in his wheelchair

Why, it's Anthony and Chrissy. Come in my dears—come in.

Chrissy pushes the chair into the room

Anthony Oh, we didn't know you were so busy. We won't keep you a moment.

Sir Annie and I are just going...

Chrissy We just wanted to say—we didn't realize there would be such a muddle about the church and you're giving us the reception anyway— so we'll settle for the registry office.

Sir Well, wherever it is, we shall be happy to lend every support—though I suspect Annie was quite looking forward to being one of the oldest bridesmaids in the business.

Annie Accompanied by a geriatric "father of the bride".

Chrissy But what we actually came to say—just to Sister Wyn—but now you are all here—it would be nice to say it to everyone—don't you think so, Anthony?

Anthony Yes, I do.

Chrissy We've thought since—if it could have happened, in this place, where everyone had made it possible for—for us to be together, there might have come a—(*she falters*) come a time...

Anthony When things built up—and we felt we weren't going to make it...

Chrissy And then perhaps we would have remembered that day—and been able to start again.

Sister Winifred turns abruptly to the window and stands with her back to the room. There is a little silence

Anthony And now we've been horribly and over-poweringly sentimental—and—and yuckish—and made you all feel very uncomfortable.

There is a very brief pause. Then Annie goes to them and holds out her hand to Anthony

Annie Speaking for myself, I am very proud and gratified and thank you both.

She kisses Chrissy and moves behind Anthony's chair

Sir Well done, my old war-horse.

Matron glances over at Sister Winifred for a second

Matron (*gently*) I am sure we all agree with Sister Annie, and she could not have better expressed our thoughts.

Sir And after her colourful and operatic outburst—how are you, Anthony, I haven't seen you for a couple of days.

Anthony Battling along, Sir. Battling on.

Sir And how is Chrissy progressing with her training as a professional nurse?

Chrissy I'm getting used to it.

Anthony I confess I'm lagging behind a bit, but I'll get there in time.

Sir I know it's not a pleasant situation, but I've always found that if you can look a problem long enough and hard enough in the face, the day will come when it stops looking back at you.

Chrissy Oh, thank you, Sir. We'll remember that.

Anthony So if you'll excuse us—we're going down to the village—to try and order a book on glass cutting.

Matron (*coming down* C) Glass cutting?

Anthony Yes. I heard about it recently. It sounds interesting. (*He laughs*) Following in your footsteps, Sir. Cutting things to pieces and putting them together again.

Sir (*laughing*) As long as you don't steal Annie to pick up the splinters.

Chrissy wheels Anthony to the door

Anthony Goodbye everybody. And once again—thank you.

There is a chorus of goodbyes. Sir opens the door for the chair

Anthony and Chrissy exit

Sir closes the door after them. He turns back into the room, smiling

Sir They'll do.
Matron I think they will.

Sir turns to Annie

Sir Oh, beauteous one—I will now take you to lunch in the village, where—since we are working this afternoon, we will consume quantities of mineral water. Let us face the arena of life in the country where dog eats dog and man devours everything. (*He puts an arm around her and makes a dramatic gesture towards the door*) Come, my love, my bride—let us to the lion and the life beyond.

Annie Yah!

Annie sweeps out past him

Sir turns in the doorway

Sir Matron, I will, if convenient, start your ward rounds about four thirty.

I only have two theatre tasks this afternoon. Both of which—and not to boast—I could do in half an hour with my eyes shut.

Matron With the help of God—and Sister Annie.

Sir (*turning in the doorway*) Why worry God?

He goes out, smiling, and closes the door behind him

Matron Clowns.

Winifred To whom many people have cause to be grateful.

Father Barrett knocks and enters R, without waiting for an answer

Barrett I must apologise for keeping you waiting so long.

Matron Oh, Father Barrett—you must have been on the phone for hours.

Barrett Yes. And now a serious talk—a very serious talk indeed with you both. Shall we sit down…?

Matron and Sister Winifred sit as before, and Father Barrett gets the small armchair and sits between them. He glances at his watch

And I shall appreciate if you will not interrupt until I've finished. I would say Sister Winifred that especially applies to you.

Winifred Yes, Father. Of course.

Father Barrett leans back in his chair

Barrett I have found myself considerably concerned—as we all are— over this question of the young people's wedding.

Winifred Oh, Father, are you saying you have—some news?

Barrett (*gently*) You promised not to interrupt.

Winifred I beg your pardon.

Barrett I confess to a sleepless night, but in the early hours—strange how so often they are productive—I found how I might move one step further.

Winifred Yes.

Barrett This morning I phoned the Mother House in London and I have had a long talk with Mother General.

Winifred Oh!

Barrett At first she was firm. No. It could not be done. But, I felt I should go on a little. Mother General is very old, but she is a person of tremendous strength and understanding. (*He laughs suddenly*) I think our younger generation might describe her as a very shrewd cookie.

They all laugh quietly

The problem, Sister Winifred, is simply and solely with you.

Winifred With me? But I only... You mean—with my wayward spirit.

Barrett (*looking at Matron*) You've told her?

Matron Yes.

Barrett Mother General understands you extremely well, Sister. She knows how you rush into things, how you are so often filled with a burning—and if you will forgive my saying so—sometimes a very inconvenient zeal.

Winifred But, Father——

Barrett She also understands—as we all do—that if this problem is not solved as you wish, you will be—to say the least—cast down.

Winifred I shall not lose my faith, if that is what you mean.

Barrett No, that is taken for granted. Sister Winifred, you are hasty, sometimes undisciplined, and in your enthusiasm you do not stop to think. But you are in this instance more than fortunate. I'd even go so far as to say you are blessed.

Winifred Blessed?

Barrett Mother General has given you *carte blanche*.

Winifred Whatever do you mean?

Barrett For two weeks.

Winifred Oh, tell me, Father, tell me quickly!

Barrett For two weeks you are to solve this problem in any way you wish.

Winifred (*jumping up*) But how can I?

Barrett There you go again. Will you please let me speak!

Winifred Oh, I'm so sorry. But, Father, if you would *please* get to the point.

Barrett *Not another word.* (*He holds up a warning hand*)

She sits down at the desk again and folds her hands in front of her

Thank you. To resume. For these two weeks—and please God, Sister, you will exercise at least a modicum of tact and discretion—you may approach who you wish, in any direction you choose. For those two weeks you may—after proper and thorough research, of course, state your case. This is on the firm understanding, of course, that you do not approach the Holy Father.

Winifred They say he is a caring, understanding, and compassionate man.

Barrett Sister Winifred—if you cannot be sensible, I will go no further with this conversation.

She bows her head

And now there is the firm and unbreakable condition. What I will call the contractual terms.

She looks up again but does not speak

Now listen carefully. If at the end of the time allocated—the two weeks—you fail—and I will tell you frankly that both Mother General and myself are convinced you will fail—then you accept the situation and put it out of your mind forever.

Winifred I have—to accept defeat?

Barrett Absolutely.

Winifred (*pausing, then quickly*) I—see. Mother General is determined that my pride—that my wayward spirit—is to be humbled and destroyed forever.

Barrett (*gently*) Neither humbled nor destroyed, Sister. Just—disciplined.

There is a pause

Matron Come, Sister—what do you say?

Winifred (*slowly*) Mother General is a very shrewd cookie indeed.

Barrett You understand?

Winifred Very clearly.

Barrett And accept it?

Winifred With all my grateful heart. (*She gets up*) If you will both excuse me—I want to make a start.

Barrett Remember you only have two weeks.

Winifred If He made the entire world in seven days, I can surely do this in twice the time.

Barrett But remember, you must be prepared from the start to fail.

Winifred (*quietly*) I am prepared to recognise that possibility.

Father Barrett gets up and crosses to her, holding out his hand

Then, Sister—into battle.

She takes his hand

Winifred Father, how can I ever thank you enough. Why should you do this for me?

Barrett (*gently*) I thought ... my wayward spirit ... deserved a fighting chance.

Winifred Oh, I will fight—how I will fight—for those two children. And if I should not fail—if I should *win*—just think, Father—it will be their great day.

Barrett (*bringing his other hand over hers in a firm clasp*) No, Sister Winifred. It will be yours.

CURTAIN

SCENE 2

Sister Winifred's office

Next morning

The scene opens as before, with the telephone shrilling incessantly

Sister Winifred hurries in R, *carrying the inevitable pile of papers, which she dumps on her desk. She is not wearing her white apron*

Winifred (*picking up the receiver*) Sister Winifred. ... Yes. ... Nurse Potter? How may I help you? ... Sister Carr sent you to get a... (*pause*) Slowly, Nurse—don't get flustered. You don't know what it looks like? Sister Carr said ... "Use the eyes God gave you and don't bother me". Oh, well, she is very busy. Where are you? ... Well, you're in the right place. Just look over to the back wall and you'll see a tall green cupboard. Open it—and on the top shelf at the back you'll see a tall glass jar. ... How tall? Well, think of a marmalade jar and add on three inches. A metal top and a little rubber tube at the side. Take it down carefully

and get back to the ward. And Nurse—don't drop it, for heaven's sake—
to get another we'll probably have to fill in about six forms. Goodbye—
glad to have helped you. (*She puts down the receiver and stands for a
moment with her hands pressed to her eyes. Then she straightens up and
looks across to the top left-hand corner*) Good-morning. I shall need
your help today as you will know but I'll try not to worry you. Goodness
knows you've enough to cope with—all the Third World and these
parliament people with their poor wives—that sad one today crying her
eyes out on the front page of the *Daily Express*. So I'll just use those
words of that wonderful soldier Sir Philip Sydney—"Lord, if on this day
in the heat of the battle, I forget thee, do not thou forget me". Thank you.
(*She goes back to her desk and sits down*) Now where to start. Draw up
a plan of campaign. (*She puts the pile of papers in her desk drawer,
brings out a large writing pad and finds a pen*) There *has to be someone
somewhere*. (*Slowly*) The Vatican must have a phone number—no, no.
It is a condition and I gave my word. Now—one must start at the top and
work down. And one can't expect to be put through to the bishop—it
will have to be a secretary and a sympathetic one. So who is next to the
Holy Father. A cardinal. And below him an archbishop. Wait a moment!
The Cardinal Archbishop—the head of the whole Catholic Church in
England. Yes, now, where does he live? (*She thinks*) London—the
palace, of course. No, I don't think I'll ring there—it will probably be
crowded and noisy. Don't they have a place somewhere in the country?
Of course—*Glasswell's*—I must have a copy somewhere. (*She goes
and searches along the bookshelves*) Directory of Hospitals... Oh,
goodness—Barbara Cartland—how on earth did that get there—Oh, I
remember—old Mrs Pryor gave it to me when she left. She said I needed
a little romance in my life. Ah... (*She finds a large book and brings it
to the desk. She opens it*) Glasswell's Directory of Ecclesiastical
Establishments in the English Counties. Cardinals—there he is,
Monseigneur. Holswell House, Kilnworth, Surrey. Come on, Sister,
into battle. (*She dials a long sequence of numbers and waits*) Hullo—
is that Holswell House? Good-morning, my dear. My name is Sister
Winifred, Assistant Matron of St Leofric's Hospital, East Anglia. ...
Oh, you've heard of us—how nice. Well, I have a problem. ... A
spiritual one? Well, not exactly, but I do need guidance. ... Yes, I have
the permission of my superiors to contact you. ... I wouldn't dream of
asking to speak to his Eminence—but perhaps some kind secretary
would take some notes and pass them on to him. ... What is it about? In

a nutshell, my dear, two young people who are not Catholics want to use our hospital church for their wedding. ... No, we don't have the usual chapel, which of course would be undenominational. We have a wonderful old church built for us in the middle ages. Oh. ... You can tell me straight away that his Eminence would never sanction it. May I ask why? ... A point of law—yes I do see. Then you can't help me. ... You might be able to? Oh, how? ... Ring—or write to my own Bishop ... in East Anglia. Where does he live? ... Cavendish House, Cornford. Why, that isn't far from here. ... Yes, please—find it in *Glasswell's*. ... Oh, thank you, you've been such a help. His Eminence must find you a great support. ... You are his private personal secretary, I was put through by mistake, well, well. He certainly does move in a mysterious way, doesn't He? Goodbye, and thank you again. (*She puts down the phone*) Well, well, (*she looks up to the left*) we're off to a fine start. Please keep it up. (*She picks up the book again*) Now... (*She checks down the page*) Here we are... Cavendish House, Cornford. His Grace, Arthur Summers ... Bishop of—mmm... (*She dials and waits*) Hullo—my name is Sister Winifred, Assistant Matron of St Leo's Hospital, East Anglia. ... Oh, you've heard of us, how nice. ... Well, I know I can't expect to be put through to his Lordship himself, but perhaps he has a secretary... Really, as many as that? He *is* lucky. Do you think one of them might speak to me about a problem and then put it before the bishop? ... Yes, I have permission from my superiors ... yes—but it is rather an unusual case. Two young people here want to be married in our church. They're not Catholics. ... No, we don't have an open chapel. If we had... Well, I thought perhaps his Lordship... Oh... (*She listens*) Absolutely not. May I ask why? ... Oh, a point of law. Yes, I do understand. Well that's that. Thank you for your patience. What? ... An idea. ... Yes, of course. ... Try the surrogate bishop. Now why didn't I think of that. Do you now where he lives? ... Castleside, Bury. ... You can't promise anything— but it's worth a try. Bless you and thank you for your help. Goodbye. (*She refers to* Glasswell's *again*) Now let's find this surrogate gentleman. (*She runs her finger down the page*) Ah—here he is. Castleside... (*She taps out the number*) Hullo, Castleside? I'm Assistant Matron at St Leo's, East Anglia. ... Oh, you've heard of us—how nice. I'm beginning to think we must be quite famous. Well, I need guidance and I know I can't speak personally to his Lordship, but I thought perhaps some nice secretary might take details. ... Yes, I do have permission from my superiors. A young couple want to be married in our church here and they're not Catholics. ... Yes it is rather important. ... You'll see if anyone can help and ring me back? Oh, thank you so much. ... Yes indeed. My number is 01343 635. Oh, I'm so grateful. You can't promise? Yes, but thank you all the same. (*She puts the phone down*) Oh, if only this could be the breakthrough. (*She puts her hands to her eyes for a moment*)

There is a knock at the door R

Oh, dear (*raising her voice*) Come in.

Polly enters R, *carrying a fair-sized parcel wrapped in fancy paper with a card on top*

Polly Please, Miss—I've got a parcel for Captain Cole, Miss—and he isn't in his room.
Winifred I expect he's out with Miss Chrissy. Put it on his table. It'll be quite safe there.
Polly Yes, Miss. (*She drifts across to the door and turns*) It's a present, Miss, from me and Bert. (*She displays the card*) It says "With love from Polly and Bert".
Winifred That's nice, Polly. I'm sure he'll be very pleased.
Polly He is all right, Miss, isn't he? (*Anxiously*) He hasn't cut himself, his finger or anything?
Winifred Polly, whatever are you talking about. Now why should you think the Captain might have cut himself?
Polly It's Bert, Miss. He said—"Pol, old girl, we'll send the Captain a load of fags. The poor bleeder's got to have something".

She drifts out R

Sister Winifred puts her hands over her face for a second

Winifred Oh, dear Lord—give me patience.

The phone rings. She snatches it up

Sister Winifred. ... Oh, thank you—yes, I was told someone might ring back. Actually, I have been on to his Eminence... Yes—the cardinal,

Holswell House. ... No, he couldn't help, so I went to the Bishop and
he passed me to the surrogate bishop and that's brought me to you. ...
(*She laughs*) Well, one has to keep trying. You have a nice voice and
sound young. May I ask your name? Brother Francis. And you are? ...
A secretary—and a trainee priest. Well, I'm Sister Winifred. ... Yes, I
do have a problem—and I do have permission to try and find someone
who can help. ... Yes, we have been nursing a young Army Captain for
over a year—terrible spinal injury. ... Yes, a mortar bomb. ... Yes,
horrific, isn't it? He has a delightful fiancee. ... Yes, yes, paraplegic. ...
Exactly. Well, we've been lucky enough to sort them out—emotion-
ally... Yes, how understanding you are—some practical help as well.
And, now they want to be married in our church here. ... Yes, it would
have been wonderful—for all of us—but that's the problem. They're
not Catholics and we have a church, not an open chapel. Brother
Francis, there must be someone somewhere—who could give permission. Could you put the details before your boss—I'm sorry, I mean his
Lordship and ask if it might be him. ... Full details—in writing—as
soon as possible. Yes—of course what exactly do you want? ... A
dossier? Yes—consisting of what? ... The young man's medical file,
yes. No problem. His Army record... Ah, where would I get that; his
commanding officer? I'll find out. ... Some information about the
young people? Their characters—are they communicants in their own
church. Dear Brother Francis, you are going to be a tower of strength,
I'll get to work at once. ... Without delay. ... Indeed and indeed. What?
(*She listens intently*) You can't promise at this stage. I know, I know—
but you are willing and caring. Oh, you are going to make the most
wonderful Cardinal Archbishop before very long. I'm convinced of it.
... Yes, right away. God bless and be with you. Thank you. Goodbye.
(*She puts down the phone*) What a very kind boy. Now, we have a tiny
crack—it must be widened—widened; start now, Sister Wyn, start now.
(*She goes to the filing cabinet and finds a long buff folder, which she
takes to her desk*) Here we are—Anthony Cole, Captain, Royal
Loamshires—oh, splendid—that gives us his regiment. (*She puts the
file on the desk and picks up the papers she has just brought in*) We'll
clear the decks—and you know where you can go for a start! (*She
crosses and dumps the papers in the basket on the little table L, then
returns to the desk*) Now—the medical file—yes. I'll send this copy. All
case histories are computerised, thank goodness. Now—the Army
record—(*she pauses, then snaps her fingers*) but of course! (*She picks*

up the phone and dials) Oh, Olive dear—something very urgent. Will
you ring the M.o.D. and get me that nice Colonel Piggot-Jones—you'll
have the number. If he's not there, leave an urgent message to ring me
back—but please, dear, keep trying—it's *so* important, and don't let
yourself be fobbed off or bullied by a Government department. ... What
do we think you are? My dear, I know exactly—the most efficient and
devoted secretary any hospital ever had—and great shall be your reward
in heaven. ... You wouldn't mind an interim dividend while you are still
on earth? My dear, you draw your dividends every day in our gratitude
and appreciation of your splendid work. (*She puts down the phone and
draws her writing pad towards her*) Ready—let's get behind the guns!
(*She pauses, looking up left*) Please, please, don't leave me now. It's
going to be a long hard fight!

CURTAIN

ACT III

SCENE 1

Sister Winifred's office

Twelve days later

Sister Winifred is sitting at her desk, signing some papers. Her white apron is hanging on a hook L. George, in uniform, is standing on her right, holding a file of papers. She finishes signing and hands him the sheet

Winifred Is that the lot, George?

George Just a couple more. (*He puts the paper in the file and places another sheet in front of her*)

As she goes to sign it, he stops her

No—not at the bottom. This one's in the top right corner.

Winifred (*dryly*) It makes a nice change. (*She signs and exchanges papers as before*) How is Anthony getting on—with his morning session. I've been off early duty for the last two days.

George Fine, just fine. But that Miss Chrissy—she's a little cracker. Pitched in at the deep end, as you might say—and never turned a hair from the word go.

Winifred Not so easy for Anthony, though.

George He's coming along. We got a laugh out of him this morning. He had one piece of luck—getting to marry a girl like that. Even if...! (*He pauses*) Sorry, Sister. I beg your pardon—but you know what I mean.

Winifred (*giving him the last signed sheet*) Yes, George. I know exactly what you mean. The fact that we take a vow of chastity doesn't mean we don't know the facts of life. Will you put those copies over there—in the big basket. (*She laughs*) When it reaches half way up the ceiling, I'm going to set fire to it.

George crosses to put the papers on top of the basket. He keeps the original file

George Send for me and I'll bring the petrol. (*He turns back and pauses by her desk*) Do you think they'll be all right, those two?

Winifred Yes, I do. We must have faith.

George Bit in short supply these days, isn't it?

Winifred Nonsense, George. Everyone has their own kind of faith. Look at you—always utterly convinced that inevitably you'll win the Pools.

George That'll be the day, Sister. That'll be the day.

He goes out laughing

Sister Winifred sits back a little wearily in her chair. She looks over and L *to the ceiling*

Winifred No. I'm not losing my faith. I shall always accept without question. But I only have two more days left. And you did say, "Not one sparrow shall fall". And these two little sparrows do need a break.

There is a knock at the door R

Oh dear! (*She pauses*) I do feel... But, the work must go on. (*She straightens herself up and calls*) Come in.

Nurse Rowlands enters R. *(NB. She should not wear her plastic apron as in Act I)*

Good-morning, Nurse. Is there something important? I am rather busy.

Rowlands Sister Carr said you would see me at half past eleven.

Winifred Oh, so she did. Yes, indeed. Please sit down. (*She indicates the opposite chair*)

Nurse Rowlands sits down

Now let's see—I should have your file somewhere. (*She finds it in her desk drawer*) Here we are. Thank goodness that was handy. (*She opens the file and refers to it*) Yes. You've been with us just six months, haven't you?

Rowlands Yes, Sister.

Winifred And I see you trained at St Phillipa's—a very good grounding. And it appears—yes—it appears you did very well.

Rowlands Thank you, Sister.

Winifred I usually have a little talk with my nurses after six months. Just to see how they're getting on.

Rowlands According to Sister Carr, I don't seem to be getting on very well.

Winifred You sound as if you don't agree.

Rowlands To be quite frank, Sister. I thought she was a little abrasive.

Winifred Well, let's see what she actually says. (*She refers to the file again—and reads*) "Nurse Rowlands has a good brain and applies herself to her work in a serious and capable manner". (*She looks up*) There's nothing wrong with that, is there?

Rowlands It's not what she said to me.

Winifred Before we go any further, we must have a few words about Sister Carr herself. I am now going to speak to you in the utmost confidence. Do I have your word that you understand and accept that.

Rowlands (*rather stiffly*) Of course.

Winifred Thank you. I know I may trust you. (*She leans back in her chair*) Sister Carr is a most highly trained and dedicated nurse. One of our most efficient and valued staff. She sets a very high standard indeed—not only for her nurses, but, for herself.

Rowlands I appreciate that, Sister, but——

Winifred Hear me out, Nurse. Then you may comment.

Rowlands I beg your pardon.

Winifred Sister Carr is married to a brute of a husband. She also has a son who is, if anything, the worst of the two. For reasons of her own, which I admit I do not understand, but which I must respect, she is utterly loyal and works hard to keep in comfort two people who are not prepared to work at all.

Rowlands But, that is terrible.

Winifred When Sister Carr goes home after a hard day's work on the ward, I do not like to think what she may have to face. Can you now realize if she sometimes may speak a little sharply?

Rowlands Thank you, Sister. I will try to understand.

Winifred And to be patient? And tolerant?

Rowlands Yes, of course.

Winifred Good. (*She picks up the file*) Now, let's see what she really does say. (*She reads*) Ah, this is the vital part, I think. (*She reads*) "Unfortunately, she has not yet learned emotional control. She is too inclined to take patients' pain upon herself and to suffer with them". (*She puts down the file*) Now that is really important.

Rowlands Surely one must show sympathy...

Winifred Compassion—yes. But always control. You cannot have tears in your eyes every time you take out a stitch or remove a dressing—does that make sense?

Rowlands Yes.

Winifred Good. (*She refers to the file again*) Ah—here we have it. (*She reads*) "Unfortunately, she gives way in a time of crisis. Last month, when young Pascoe died, I thought she would become hysterical. Fortunately, she controlled herself before I had to send her off the ward. I would not wish this situation to arise again". (*She looks up*) Is this correct?

Rowlands I am—I am very sorry...

Winifred How many times have I told you girls to use detachment. You absolutely must learn to be detached.

Rowlands Sister—how can one possibly be detached about death?

Winifred (*gently*) Because, dear child, death itself is the ultimate detachment.

Rowlands He was only twenty-eight...

Winifred Our dear Lord was only four years older when He was crucified.

Rowlands Don't—I can't bear it...

Winifred He had to. And so must we. We owe Him that—if only for that moment when the first nail went in. (*She breaks*) I'm sorry. I don't mean to preach.

Rowlands Thank you. I think I have everything quite sorted now.

Winifred Good. And, before you go, shall we say that short prayer I ask you girls to repeat each morning after early service? (*She gets up*)

Nurse Rowlands gets up too. They clasp their hands and bow their heads

Winifred ⎫
⎬ (*together*) Lord—take our hands this day and turn them to
Rowlands ⎭ your healing service.

Winifred Now off you go. Let me see, you're on St David's this week, aren't you?

Rowlands Yes.

Winifred Then you have a very busy afternoon in front of you. Three patients due for theatre——

Rowlands Oh, Sister—one last thing...

Winifred (*glancing at her watch*) Make it brief then.

Rowlands We're all very sorry—very sorry indeed—about the wedding.

Winifred Ah—the wedding.

Rowlands It does seem a shame—after—after all that's happened. Couldn't it possibly be arranged?

Winifred I'm afraid not, Nurse. And, of course you will understand I cannot discuss it with you. It is a very delicate matter of protocol.

Rowlands Yes, Sister.

Winifred Be off, then. Back to the grindstone, and imagine you're Florence Nightingale at Scutari. (*She laughs*) Do you realize that in those days they didn't have any sluices? How ever they coped with the bedpans, I simply can't imagine.

Laughing, Nurse Rowlands goes to the door R *and pauses*

Rowlands Thank you for everything.

Nurse Rowlands goes out, shutting the door

Sister Winifred sighs. She stands for a moment, then turns to look up at the left-hand corner of the room

Winifred It isn't really fair, is it? We take them when they're so young, with their heads full of clothes and cosmetics—and boyfriends, and we put them into a starched uniform and hand them the responsibilities of life and death. (*She pauses*) But You'll cope of course. You always have in the last two thousand years.

The phone rings. She picks it up quickly

Sister Winifred. … Oh, Olive—oh, please not now. I must keep my line open for a most important call. … Only a minute—oh, well then—but do be quick. (*She listens for a long moment*) Now let me see if I've got it right. The drugs list. The Department of Medicine—a mistake—they knocked off three noughts. … Well, it would indeed make a difference, wouldn't it? … Right, I'll come down before you leave and we'll really write a stiff letter to that wretched man—that Mr Sergeant. … What dear? … Yes, I do know his proper name—but I always think of him as Mr Sergeant. It's time he was reduced to the ranks. (*She puts down the phone rather sharply and leans back in her chair again*) This won't do, Sister Winifred, you're losing your grip.

There is a knock at the door R

Oh, no. (*She pulls herself upright*) Well, I suppose the routine must go on. (*She calls*) Please come in.

Brother Francis opens the door and comes in R. *He is a very personable young man in his twenties, trim and attractive in his clerical vest and long cassock. He is pulling off his wide brimmed black hat as he comes in*

Francis Sister Winifred?

Winifred (*getting up*) Yes...

Francis Your kind secretary told me where I might find you. Let me introduce myself. Brother Francis from Castleside—

Winifred Oh, Brother Francis! (*She gets up and goes to meet him* C, *holding out her hand*) How wonderful you have come in person.

Francis His Lordship thought it appropriate. He was most touched by your communication and sends you his greetings and a special blessing. (*He clasps her hand warmly*)

Winifred And I you. But forgive me—in this most joyful moment—I forgot my manners. Please sit down. (*She indicates the small armchair, takes his hat to a peg and returns*)

Francis (*sitting*) Thank you.

Winifred To send you in person can only mean one thing, oh, everybody is going to be so overjoyed.

Francis Sister——

Winifred No—don't tell me. I want the young people to know before anyone. Let me send for them. (*She picks up the phone*) Sister Winifred. This is important. Will someone please go straight away and find Anthony and Chrissy. Usually at this time they'll be down by the lake. ... Yes—tell them I have a very special visitor and they must come immediately. (*She puts down the phone*) It may take a little time. While we are waiting, would you like a cup of coffee?

Francis That's a splendid idea—thank you.

Winifred Sister Appolline, our cook, is a jewel. If she was in private life she would have the finest restaurant in London— (*she dials on the phone as she speaks*) and probably a fortune in guaranteed income bonds. (*Into the phone*) Is that the kitchen? ... Oh, Sister Appolline. Now, I have a very special guest here—Brother Francis—from Castleside. ... Yes indeed, from his Lordship himself. Could you send us over a pot of your superb coffee? ... To my office—yes. ... Hold on. (*She turns to Brother Francis*) How do you like it?

Francis Tell her the classic answer to that. As hot as hell, as black as night, as sweet as love.

Winifred (*into the phone*) He says... Oh, you heard that. (*She turns to Brother Francis*) She said that is how it will come. And, Sister, have you by chance any of those little cinnamon biscuits? ... You have? Then please—just a few. Thank you. What? ... (*To Brother Francis*) She says are you staying for lunch?

Francis I should be delighted to be asked.

Winifred (*into the phone*) He is invited. Will you do something extremely special—even for you? (*She listens and laughs*) You're fresh out of peacocks? So what...? (*She listens again*) A rainbow trout ... poached in white wine ... with a basil sauce ... creamed potatoes ... and a fruit salad for dessert. (*She turns to Brother Francis*) How do you feel about that?

Francis It must surely be a case of love at first bite.

Winifred (*into the phone*) You heard that, too? Dear Sister Appolline— you shall have a halo of peacocks' wings. (*She replaces the receiver*)

Francis This is going to be a day of delight. I must, of course, see Matron before I leave.

Winifred I will take you to her when you have seen the young people. In any case, she will join you at lunch.

Francis So tell me a little more about Anthony. You have straightened out some of the problems I believe.

Winifred Yes. Of course—he has taken it very hard...

Francis Naturally—poor boy.

Winifred Brother Francis—I—had to break him down—I did not enjoy it—to agree to the marriage. I hope I have done the right thing.

Francis I feel sure you have. And the girl?

Winifred Is loving and loyal and will, I hope and pray, support him. We are giving her some training here—with the person she'll be nursing.

Francis How splendid.

Winifred And now with this marriage here—which they have set their hearts on...

Francis Sister, tell me something. When this was first vetoed, did you not think of one solution—very simple, and, one might say, desirable.

Winifred You mean the possibility of—their conversion.

Francis Yes.

Winifred It was the first thing that came into my mind—I discussed it at some length with Father Barrett.

Francis Father Barrett?

Winifred He is our chaplain. And of course my spiritual advisor—and a great friend.

Francis And?

Winifred We both realize they are in a state of very—considerable emotion—and might well have consented.

Francis Then?

Winifred We both agreed we could not commit ourselves to spiritual blackmail.

Francis A good and wise decision.

Winifred And—now you have come to set the seal on everything.

There is a knock at the door

Come in.

Polly enters R, *carefully balancing a silver tray, with a silver coffee pot, cream jug, cups and saucers, and a plate of biscuits*

Polly Please, Miss...

Winifred Come in, Polly.

Brother Francis jumps up

Francis Polly, is it? Let me take that. (*He takes the tray from her and puts it on the desk*)

She stares at him, fascinated

Winifred Polly, this is Brother Francis. He has come to see Anthony and Chrissy—about the wedding.

Polly goes up to him and stares at him. Suddenly she bends her knee and makes a little bob of a curtsy, holding out her hand

Polly Good-morning, sir...

Winifred Why, Polly...

Brother Francis shakes hands with Polly

Francis Good-morning to you, Polly. And do you live here at St Leo's?

Polly Oh yes, sir. (*Importantly*) I'm a maid. I do the trays and the laundry and take papers to Miss Olive. Are you going to marry the Captain and Miss Chrissy?

Francis No, Polly. I'm only learning. (*He laughs*) You might say I'm still at school.

Polly I was at school once. In London. It was horrid and I was very unhappy. And then Sister brought me here and I'm happy all the time.

Winifred We regard Polly as one of our sparrows.

Francis How splendid. (*To Polly*) I hope you will be happy every day for all your life.

Polly Oh, thank you, sir. You *are* kind. Could I—could I do something for you, sir? I would like to do something for you.

Winifred Polly——

Francis Well, perhaps you would like to pour me a cup of coffee?

Polly Oh yes, sir! (*She goes to the tray*) Do you take sugar and the cream, sir?

Francis Just plain coffee, thank you.

She pours a cup and takes it to him

Thank you. (*He drinks the coffee*)

Polly (*watching intently*) Is it good, sir? Sister Appolline makes it special. She'll want to know——

Francis It's very good indeed.

Polly And the biscuits, sir. (*She fetches the plate*) They're special, too. (*She offers the plate with both hands*)

Francis (*taking a biscuit*) I can see they are. Would you like to take one for yourself?

Polly Oh no, thank you, sir. I don't eat biscuits, any more. Bert don't like cr——

Winifred (*breaking in quietly*) Polly, that will do. Go back to work now. You can come for the tray later.

Polly Yes, Miss. And please, Miss, Sister Appolline says lunch is in exactly half an hour. And you're not to be late—because good food is given to us by—(*she remembers*) by grace and—and favour. And not to be kept waiting.

Winifred Thank you Polly. Away you go.

Polly Yes, Miss. Goodbye, sir. (*She puts the biscuits on the tray*)

Francis Goodbye, Polly. You're a very kind little girl. God bless you.

Polly Thank you, Sir. (*She stands staring at him for a moment. Then she turns to Sister Winifred*) Oh, Miss—aren't he lovely? If it weren't for Bert, I could eat him.

She goes out R, shutting the door behind her. Brother Francis splutters into his coffee cup

Winifred You will never, as long as you live, get a more sincere compliment.

Francis Very obviously one of your successes, Sister.

Winifred (*smiling*) We are very happy—and privileged—to think so.

Brother Francis pulls out his handkerchief and wipes his lips, then gets up and puts his coffee cup on the tray. He indicates the pot

Francis This coffee is superb. May I?

Winifred Please do. Here, let me. (*She pours another cup and gives it to him*)

Father Barrett enters quickly R

Barrett Sister... (*He pauses*) Oh, I beg your pardon. I had hoped to find you alone.

Winifred You have come at a very wonderful moment. This is Brother Francis. He has come specially to see us. From Castleside.

Barrett Castleside. Then...

Winifred Yes. From the bishop. Oh, Father, he has brought his Lordship's permission!

Francis Sister...

Winifred Brother Francis—our chaplain, Father Barrett. He obtained permission for me to work towards this wonderful day.

Brother Francis puts his cup on the tray and holds out his hand

Francis How do you do, sir?

The two men shake hands. Sister Winifred pours another cup of coffee

We have, of course, heard of your wonderful work, but I did not realize your setting was so beautiful. And that church—it is magnificent. (*He turns up to the window and looks out*)

Father Barrett follows him, standing on his left

Barrett Yes, a great legacy from our great founder.

Sister Winifred takes a cup of coffee over to Father Barrett. There is a knock at the door R. Sister Winifred turns

Winifred Come in.

Chrissy enters R, pushing Anthony in his wheelchair. She moves straight across and brings him LC, facing the main door. Anthony speaks as they cross

Anthony I'm sorry we've been so long in coming——

Father Barrett crosses R and shuts the door, returning to the window, where he stands drinking his coffee

Winifred My dears, I want you to meet Brother Francis—from Castleside. He has come straight from the bishop himself—to bring you the wonderful news.

Anthony |
            | (*together*) News?
Chrissy |

Winifred Yes. I have not allowed him to tell me officially. You must be the very first to know. (*She turns to Brother Francis*) Brother Francis— tell them. Tell them the news we all want to know!

Brother Francis pauses. He goes and puts his coffee cup down on the tray. He turns to face Anthony and Chrissy

Francis Anthony, my dear boy.

They shake hands and he turns to Chrissy

And Chrissy. (*He shakes her hand also*) I bring you a personal message

from his Lordship. He commends your courage, Anthony, and sends a
special blessing to you both.

Anthony Please thank him from us——

Winifred And now—tell them!

*There is a slight pause. Brother Francis turns so that he stands by
Anthony's chair*

Francis My dears—I am so sorry—so very sorry——

Winifred Brother Francis!

Francis I am saddened to have to tell you—the answer is no.

There is a silence

(*Gently*) I did try to tell you, Sister.

Winifred Yes, you did. Oh, why am I always so hasty, so precipitate?

Chrissy But, why? We did think, perhaps——

Francis It is a very rigid rule and cannot be set aside. Are you so very
disappointed?

Chrissy Yes, we are. We felt it would really set the seal on everything for
the future.

Francis Come now, let us discuss this objectively. Does it really matter
so much?

Anthony It matters to us.

Francis But think for a moment. You are going to be married—that, in
itself, is a brave undertaking—and you will need much courage—I
know—to face it. But you will, wherever you are, be married in the sight
of God, which is the important thing. Because He is everywhere—not
just in St Leo's great church—but wherever you are. Why, at this very
moment—do you realize—he is here in this very room.

Winifred Brother Francis!

Francis Yes, Sister?

Winifred If we had the usual open chapel, instead of St Leo's church—
that—chapel would have allowed it—what does it say? "Open to
everyone—class, race or creed"? *Yes?*

Francis Yes, but...

Winifred Then for this day—this one short space of time—this room may
be a chapel, filled with the loving presence of God himself.

Chrissy clasps her hands together. There is a pause

Francis (*quietly*) Sister Winifred—I think—I believe—you may have the answer.

Chrissy Oh, Anthony...

Winifred Does it have to be authenticated? Where would we apply?

Francis I will ask his Lordship.

Winifred Now!

Francis Yes—now. Where may I find a phone? I would prefer to speak privately—you understand...

Winifred (*indicating* L) In there—the extension. Oh, Brother Francis—hurry!

Brother Francis pauses for a moment, looking at them all. Then he runs off L, shutting the door behind him

Sister Winifred bows her head into her hands for a moment. Then she looks up

Everything will have to be altered—changed around. Of course—and what a joy to do it. Let me see—a small altar in front of the windows—and build it up higher and then drape it. I think I know where——

Barrett And——

Winifred And we shall need a cross. Maybe we can borrow the small one from the side chapel—and some vases—we must have flowers——

Barrett And an organ. No—perhaps there won't be room for that.

Winifred Of course there will be room. We can use the little portable piano/organ that we use for Christmas carols round the wards——

Chrissy And——

Winifred We can put it in the corridor just outside—there will be plenty of space along the wall—and we can leave the door open—and Sister Freda will do the rest. (*She clasps her hands*) Oh, don't you see how it is all coming together!

There is a knock at the door R

Come in.

George enters R

George Excuse me, Sister...

Winifred Yes, George. What is it?

George I've been looking all over for the Captain. May I have a word.

Winifred Of course.

George Well, sir… A message from Simmy. Can you meet him round about six by the main garage. He's been working on Miss Chrissy's car—and he wants to see if you can use the switches for working the ramp.

Anthony Thank you very much, George. Six o'clock it is.

George And Captain—is it true that a young man has come from the bishop to say you can be married here after all?

Winifred How the news travels. Well, not quite, George. Certainly not in the church—but we are asking if this room may be used as a chapel—just for the day.

George Blimey, what an idea. (*He looks round*) But it'll have to be taken apart somewhat, won't it?

Winifred Yes, but everyone will help. I am sure everyone—will help…

George Of course we will. Cor! What a lark—a real St Leo's wedding!

Anthony (*suddenly*) George—how would you like to be my best man?

George Your…?

Anthony Best man. One of my friends was invited, but I've just heard he's been transferred up north. Oh, come on, George—what about it?

George Well…

Anthony Come to think of it—who better? You've looked after me, day and night for twelve months. Come on—see me to rights for the last time.

Chrissy Oh yes, George. Please do!

George Well, I've never done it before. What exactly would I have to do?

Anthony Give me an extra close shave, get me in my uniform, bring me over to the altar in time—and make sure we haven't forgotten the ring.

George By jingo, sir—I'll do it. For you and Miss Chrissy—I'm blest if I don't.

Chrissy Oh, thank you, George. (*She jumps up and gives him a hug and a kiss*)

There is a murmur of general approval

George I've got to be going. I'll tell Simmy you'll be there, sir. Oh, and Sister Appolline has got flames coming out of the top of her head. She wants you all with your bibs on right away. (*He picks up the coffee tray and moves to the door* R) Best man—what a snorter!

He goes out R

Simultaneously, Brother Francis rushes in L, *beaming*

Francis It's all arranged! It's all arranged!

There is a joyful chorus

Barrett			God be praised.
Winifred			Glory be to God.
Anthony	*(together)*		Chrissy—darling.
Chrissy			Oh, how wonderful.

Chrissy and Anthony hug each other

Barrett Sister Winifred—you have won! You have won your fight.

She looks at him steadily for a moment

Winifred (*gently*) Yes, I think maybe I have.

Francis Sister Winifred, his Lordship was enchanted—quite enchanted—
at the idea. He gives his consent with delight, and sends more prayers
for the day. There will obviously be some small formalities, but we will
see to those for you at Castleside. Of course, children, you must now see
the incumbent of your choice and arrange for the banns. Or would you
like me to…?

Anthony No, thank you, Brother Francis. We will see the vicar in the
village. He is a good soul—he will come.

Francis Oh, and one thing. His Lordship makes a condition.

Winifred A condition?

Francis Well, not a condition exactly. He said—a favour for a favour.

Winifred Whatever he asks, we will so joyfully do.

Francis He would like someone to be present from Castleside. To bring
a final blessing from him to everyone there. And… (*He looks round at
them, smiling*) And he has suggested that someone might be me.

There is a delighted chorus of approval

Winifred Off you all go, now. Brother Francis, I would like to see you

before you finally leave. And you will give his Lordship our over-
whelming thanks—and send him our blessing in return.

Francis Thank you.

Winifred Anthony and Chrissy, please take Brother Francis to Matron's
office. And then you may all go over to lunch.

Francis Are you lunching with us, sir?

Barrett No—you must excuse me. I have—things to do.

Chrissy starts to move behind the chair. Father Barrett stops her

Here—let me help you. (*He moves behind Anthony's chair*)

Brother Francis collects his hat and moves R *to open the door. Father
Barrett, Anthony and Chrissy cross* R

Chrissy goes out with Brother Francis

*Father Barrett pushes the chair out into the corridor. He turns in the
doorway*

Are you not coming to lunch?

Winifred No. I am on duty in ten minutes. (*She moves to him*) Oh,
Father—we have achieved it. I have won—say you are pleased I have
won.

Barrett Of course—and you deserved it.

Winifred I couldn't have done it without you.

Barrett You must excuse me now. We will talk later.

Winifred Oh yes. Please—there is so much to arrange.

He nods and goes out

*She pauses, then suddenly turns, looking up at the left-hand corner. Her
face lights up. She raises her clasped hands*

Oh—well done! Well done!

CURTAIN

SCENE 2

Sister Winifred's office

Six weeks later. Early in the morning

Because of a major set change during this act, where a long interval is not convenient, this scene has been specially constructed so that the entire set change takes place before the audience. It is suggested that two of the backstage staff are asked to participate. They do not have to speak. They should both be male—if possible—and wear either long brown holland coats or jeans and black shiny jackets. In either case, these should be stencilled on the back in large letters "St Leo's", which explains everything to the audience immediately without the use of dialogue. Any necessary dialogue is spoken by George or Brother Francis

When the curtain rises, the change is in full swing. The desk has been pushed down C *and the phone unplugged, on the floor beside it*

Both George and Brother Francis are in shirtsleeves rolled to the elbow. George wears dark trousers and a snowy white shirt, a stiff white collar, and a red bow tie with white spots. His dark jacket is hung on one of the wall hooks L

Brother Francis wears black trousers and his clerical vest and collar. His long black cassock and his black hat are hung on the hook beside George's jacket

George and one of the helpers are carrying the filing cabinet off R. *Brother Francis and the other helper are moving the bookcase off* L

George A bit more to your right, Ben—easy does it.

They ease the cabinet through the door and he continues speaking off stage

(*Off*) Along to the end and flat against the wall. Hullo, Sister Freda— mind your back. ... Yes we'll move your organ next. Where—just a bit further along? ... How's that? Good. ... More light. On the keyboard—

no problem—hold on. See if this flex will reach, Ben—plug's on the wall just there. Good. Switch on. Fine. How's that, Sister? ... Well give us a sample—just to make sure.

There is a little outbreak of music—not religious—but bright (and not pop)

(*Off*) Anything more while we're here? ... Good.

George enters, followed by the helper

Brother Francis comes in L

Francis Next?
George We'll leave that little table—it'll be useful. But you might take out that big basket. I don't think Sister will want to see that today.
Francis Right.

Brother Francis goes off L *with the basket of papers*

George turns back to the other helper

George Now we'll sort out the chairs. We want two along by that wall. (*He indicates* R) Take those round the desk, that'll be three. (*He calls*) Brother Francis.
Francis (*off* L) Yes!
George We need another upright chair. There's one by the window.
Francis Right...

George and the helper move the chairs. They put the two arms below the door R, *and the straights below the door* L

George That's it—arms for Matron and Sister—straights for the two winners in the draw.

Brother Francis comes in L *with a small upright chair*

Francis Do we know who they are?
George Not yet. Matron said wait till the very last minute because so

many will have to be disappointed. (*He takes the chair from Brother Francis and hands it to the helper*)

While George and Brother Francis are talking, the helper lines up the four chairs neatly against the wall. See plan at the end of the script

Francis But all the others will be in the church listening to our relay from here. It's all fixed up?

George Yes. The engineers finished and checked everything by eight o'clock. It was Father Barrett's idea, you know.

The other helper enters L, carrying a large square cardboard box neatly covered with a purple cloth. It is obviously heavy

Thanks, Charley. On the little table there—that's right.

The helper puts the box on the table

Thanks. That's about it, then. Except the cross. (*He turns to Brother Francis*) Is it here?

Francis I brought it myself. It's in the church porch.

George Thanks, Charley.

The helpers come C

Just the cross now. It's in the church porch. Mind how you go. It might be a bit heavy. But you'll manage with that small trolley. You might as well bring it straight back. By the time you've been over and loaded and brought it back, we'll be near enough ready.

The two helpers nod and go out R

George turns to Brother Francis

Now for the big one.

He and Brother Francis move to the desk. George sweeps the pens, papers, etc. from the desktop into one of the drawers. Taking an end each, they move it directly under the window, making sure it is absolutely straight

I'll get the cover.

George goes out L

Brother Francis carefully adjusts the curtains behind the desk, then takes the phone to the table UL *and plugs it into the wall socket*

George returns R, *carrying an armful of folded purple cloth*

This won't take a minute. Simmy measured it all meticulously and stood over Sister Freda while she ran it up on the sewing machine.

Brother Francis helps him spread it out, a neat fitted cover, with a plain top and a pleated or frilled skirt

Just ease it over. The top's padded and it should fit perfectly.

They fit the cover neatly over the desk, adjusting the skirts so that the folds reach neatly and evenly just to the floor

Francis Excellent. Good for Simmons.

George fetches the box from the little table

George This weighs a ton—can you give us a hand?

Brother Francis helps to lift and place it in the centre of the draped desk. They align it carefully to be central

Simmy made this specially firm to take the weight of the cross. (*He laughs*) Did you know he actually rang up Castleside to ask?
Francis No. They never told me. I wonder who he got hold of?
George Apparently he sweet-talked the young lady who answered the phone. She found out for him and rang back.
Francis Well, he's certainly got a way with him. And there seems nothing he can't do with his hands.
George (*laughing*) You can say that again! If you want confirmation of that, just ask Nurse Potter.

The two helpers return R, *carrying between them a handsome brass cross, about three feet high*

That's it, lads. Over here. In the centre—right on top of the box—

They set the cross carefully in place, steadying it and aligning it up. They all stand back to look

How's that, sir?

Francis Couldn't be better.

George Good lads. Here... (*He pulls an envelope from his pocket and hands it to one of them*) The Captain asked me to say thank you. So we'll see you later. And, you'll be well looked after. He's already sent up four crates of beer.

The two men laugh, wave and go out R

George turns back to Brother Francis, who is standing before the little altar

Looks really good, doesn't it?

Francis Yes, George. Really good. (*He takes a couple of steps back and bows his head to the cross, then turns down L*)

George hesitates, then goes to the altar, glances over his shoulder, and gives an embarrassed little nod of his head towards the cross

Sister Winifred enters R, carrying a silver vase in each hand, both full of beautiful roses

Winifred Good-morning, gentlemen... (*She stops as she sees the altar*) Oh! How beautiful. How very good and clever of you. May I... (*She places a vase on each side of the cross*) I think it will take the flowers. (*She stands back for a second and bows her head. She turns to face Brother Francis*) You really have done admirably.

Francis Show her the finale, George. Throw the switch.

George reaches behind the dark crimson curtains. There is a click and the whole altar area is suddenly bathed in soft golden light. Sister Winifred clasps her hands

Winifred Perfect!

The soft chime sounds the quarter

George Oh, my gawd—excuse me, Sister. But there's the quarter. I must go and fetch the Captain. (*He takes down his jacket and is struggling into it as he speaks*) He wants to be here well before...

Winifred How is he this morning?

George A bit quiet. Dr O'Connell sent over some tablets—just in case— but he won't take nothing. Says he'll be fine when he's got a couple of glasses of champers under his belt. And, that reminds me—Bert gave me some more telegrams. (*He pulls envelopes out of his pocket and gives them to Brother Francis*) Excuse me—I gotta dash.

George exits quickly R

Francis (*turning over the envelopes*) Two for Anthony—and a letter for you, Sister. (*He gives her an envelope and takes the others to the little table L*)

Winifred For me? (*She looks at the envelope*) Oh, this is from Father Barrett. How very kind... (*She smiles and folds the envelope, putting it in her pocket*)

Francis Am I right in thinking that he made an essential contribution to this day?

Winifred One might say he—made it possible.

Francis May I say here, Sister—that I am most impressed—and moved— by the great outpouring of sympathy—and practical help—St Leo's has given to these two young people.

Winifred How could it be otherwise. Anthony has been here so long— and so courageous. And little Chrissy has fought so bravely. How could we not take them to our hearts.

Francis Sentiment is not well regarded nowadays.

Winifred If sentiment is an expression of love for one's fellow man— then I see no wrong in it. I am glad you are here today, Brother Francis. When shall you give us his Lordship's special messages?

Francis One for the young people at the end of their service. The other— with Matron's permission—at the end of the day when everyone is present.

Winifred That will be much appreciated.

George returns R, wheeling Anthony in his chair. Anthony is resplendent in his full officer's uniform, with braided cap and a small swagger stick on his knee

Anthony Good-morning, Sister Wyn—Brother Francis.

Winifred My dear boy! How are you feeling?

Anthony Great. And what a wonderful arrangement you've made. It looks absolutely marvellous.

Winifred And so do you. I don't know whether to curtsy or stand to attention.

They all laugh happily

George Sir, I'll just take you over—facing the door. People will be popping in and out. Then—at the last moment—I'll put you ready for Miss Chrissy. (*He takes the wheelchair across the stage*) Excuse me, Sister. (*He passes her and positions Anthony* L, *half facing the audience. He goes and stands leaning on the back of the chair during the following conversations*)

Anthony Is Chrissy here yet?

Winifred Since ten o'clock. Sir brought her down as arranged—and handed her straight over to Sister Annie—so you need have no worries there.

Anthony Thank you.

Winifred We had a few words when she came in. (*Quietly*) She sent you her love. (*She glances at her watch*) It won't be long now. Are you sure you're all right—is there anything anyone can do for you?

Anthony (*laughing*) Nothing while I have George.

Winifred Then I have promised to give Matron a few minutes—just to sign some urgent forms. Even on a day like this, that wretched little man can't leave us in peace. (*She takes Anthony's hand*) God bless and be with you, my dear.

Brother Francis takes his hat from the peg and crosses to open the door R

Francis And I've promised to go to the village and pick up the vicar. After you, dear lady.

Sister Winifred gives Anthony's hand a last reassuring clasp, then goes out R, *passing Brother Francis, who follows her, closing the door after them*

Anthony (*reaching out to touch one of the roses on the altar*) It is quite incredible how kind everyone is. St Leo's is really doing us proud, George.

George Of course, we're proud of you—and Miss Chrissy. Now—you're sure you're all right, sir? Anything I can do for you, anything at all—while there's still time? I know you don't want Dr O'Connell's pills—so I took the liberty of bringing a little stiffener in my pocket.

Anthony No, George—thank you all the same. (*He leans back in his chair*)

George fetches one of the upright chairs from below door L and brings it to the right side of Anthony's chair. He sits down so that they are companionably together

Just look at this room, George. What everyone has done for us. I'll never be able to thank them enough.

George Yes, you will, Captain. You'll know just what to do when the time comes. The notes for your speech are in your right-hand pocket, and I've checked I've got the ring. Everything's organised—nothing more to worry about.

Anthony It's—very peaceful—here.

George So it is, sir. So it is. So you just sit quiet for a minute or two—and sort of charge up your batteries, and then I read you those telegrams.

Anthony Good idea, George. Good idea. (*He leans back in his chair*)

There is a little silence

(*Suddenly*) George...

George Yes, Captain.

Anthony (*quietly*) Thank you for everything.

George You've nothing to thank me for, sir.

Anthony Oh no? A year, every morning, every night—often during the day—always there—ready—except when you were off duty. And I've often thought, you sometimes weren't off duty when you should have been.

George I'm going to miss you, sir.

Anthony I'm going to miss you, George. Like hell, I am.

George But, it's all going to be different now—you got Miss Chrissy. Believe me, sir—you couldn't have done better.

Anthony I know. I know. And George—promise me—we'll keep in touch—

George I'd like that. And Captain—you promise me—if there's ever anything I can do for you and Miss Chrissy—anything at all—you just ring us here and I'll be straight on my way, whether I'm on duty or not.

Anthony With Fanny Carr chasing you up on a broomstick.

George And that's a promise.

Anthony Yes. And now, will you just read me those telegrams before I have to wheel myself over and read them myself.

George Yes, Captain—right now. (*He fetches the telegrams and stands on Anthony's right*) There's two. These look official, Captain—this one says (*he reads*) "Good on you, Anthony boy, tell Chrissy we all love her too". It's signed "'C' Company. Aldershot".

Anthony (*laughing*) That's the lads. Bless 'em all. Next.

George Very formal this one, sir. (*He reads*) "Warmest personal wishes and regards to you both. Darren Piggot-Jones".

Anthony Well! Well! Porker. The old man himself. We'll have to send him a bit of wedding cake. Take those for me, George. And see I get them before I leave. All of them—and there seems to be a sackful—have to be answered.

George Yes, sir. (*He pockets the telegrams and looks at his watch*) Time's getting on, Captain. Now, are you absolutely sure there's nothing——

Anthony George—don't fuss.

George But...

Anthony George! (*Deliberately*) Bang to rights!

George Sorry, Captain. I'm not with you.

Anthony Then you should be. Oh, for God's sake, George—you must know. Every morning, almost without fail, for all that time...

George Sir?

Anthony Every morning—when you've got me cleaned up—and dressed—and ready in my chair for the day—what have you always said? "There you are, Captain. Bang to rights". So I'm saying it to you now, George. Bang to rights.

George (*suddenly*) Why, that's it, sir. So it is. Bang to rights. Well, well... Bang to rights.

There is a knock at the door R

Anthony Better see who that is, George.

George crosses R *and opens the door*

Nurse Rowlands enters, very smart and trim, and made-up

Rowlands Is this the right place? (*She breaks off as she sees Anthony and runs to his chair*) Oh, Anthony, I've come to your wedding. Look, I won a ticket in the draw. (*She shows him the piece of pasteboard*)

Anthony Rowley—how splendid. I'm so glad. (*He pulls her down to kiss her*) Who won the other ticket—do we know?

Rowlands No. I wasn't at the actual draw. Someone just left this in my room. (*She suddenly pulls out her handkerchief*)

Anthony Why—what's this? Come on, love. We don't want any tears today.

Sister Winifred enters R *with Matron behind her*

Winifred Nurse Rowlands. What are you doing here?

Rowlands (*holding out the ticket*) I won this...

Winifred Then what are you crying for? Come here. (*She moves Nurse Rowlands* C)

Matron crosses and speaks to Anthony. George crosses to move his chair back below the door L

Rowlands It's so—so sad...

Winifred It's *not* sad. It is a day of great joy. Now wipe your eyes and go and sit on that chair at the end of the row. And don't let me see another single tear. Understood?

Rowlands Thank you, Sister. I'll be all right now. (*She goes and sits on the chair below the door* L)

George moves over behind Anthony again. The door opens suddenly

Polly comes in, stopping just inside. She wears a long flowered dress and her hair is elaborately gathered on top of her head and garnished with a large blue bow. She is wildly excited

Winifred Polly!

Polly I've come to the wedding! I've come to see the Captain married!

Sister Winifred crosses to her

Winifred Polly—what are you doing?

Polly This is me best dress, and Sister Carr's done me hair—only she's not sure about the bow—please, Miss—is me bow all right?

Winifred Polly, you can't...

Polly Yes I can! I've got me prize... I've won me ticket. Here. (*She shows a piece of pasteboard similar to Nurse Rowlands'*) I've won me draw.

Winifred Now, Polly.

Polly But please, Miss. Bert says I've to be ever so quiet and not cry. And he says I'm not to go charging up to kiss the Captain.

Winifred I should think not!

Polly But—I did want to kiss the Captain (*the last words are a wail*) on his wedding day... (*Her face crumples*)

Winifred Polly, if you shed as much as one tear, you will—ticket or no ticket—go over to the church with all the others.

Matron goes over to them

Matron Sister...

Anthony (*breaking in*) Matron—Sister. Please—a word...

Matron Of course.

Anthony Polly...

She looks at him and gives a big sniff

Polly, come here. (*He holds out both hands to her*)

She hesitates, looking at Sister Winifred and Matron

Come here.

She goes slowly to his chair and takes his hands. He pulls her down to him and very gently kisses her first on one cheek and then on the other

Polly (*overcome*) Oh, sir. And Bert did say...

Anthony (*laughing*) So you just tell Bert it's all right. You didn't kiss the Captain. The Captain kissed you.

Polly Oh, sir... (*Her face crumples again*)

Winifred Polly, will you please stop wailing; you're a very lucky girl. Now, just go over there by Nurse Rowlands, and don't say another word. Do you understand—not another word!

Polly Yes, Miss. Thank you, Miss. (*She goes meekly to the chair next to Nurse Rowlands, where she sits obviously telling her all about it*)

Sister Winifred moves C. *Matron follows her*

Matron Sister Winifred—this isn't like you. And this day of all days. Is anything wrong?

Winifred I will not have hysteria. And you know how it can spread...

Matron I am sure——

Winifred And when I think of the time and planning and effort and—and yes—I *will* say it—the love, which has been lavished on this day. I will not—I will *not*—see it all washed away on a tide of salt water!

Matron Steady, Sister, dear. The Wayward Spirit must not go against the wind today.

Winifred I am sorry. (*She calms down*) Please forgive me. I am—all right now.

Matron (*gently*) I understand, Sister. Believe me—everything is going to be splendid.

There is a sudden soft outbreak of some religious music off R. *Matron turns*

And something appears to be happening.

Brother Francis and the Vicar enter R. *The Vicar is an impressive elderly man, ready in his cassock, surplice and stole. He has a head of thick white hair and a trim beard. He carries a large prayer book under his arm*

Brother Francis goes straight across L *and hangs his hat back on the peg. He stands behind Anthony's chair, talking to him and George. While he does this, Matron goes and greets the Vicar*

Good-morning, Vicar. I don't think you have met my Assistant Matron, Sister Winifred.

The Vicar and Sister Winifred shake hands. Matron indicates Nurse Rowlands and Polly

Nurse Rowlands and Polly—members of staff.

*He shakes hands with them both, Polly making her little bent knee bob.
Matron brings the Vicar over to Anthony*

Anthony you know. This is George—one of our nurses who has
Anthony in his special care.

*He shakes hands with them both. They chat together. A soft strain of music
suddenly sounds outside the door. Matron crosses and opens it wide,
making sure the door goes back against the wall. The music becomes
louder. Matron turns to her seat at the end of the row. Sister Winifred sits
beside her. The music stops*

*Suddenly, Anthony's hands close hard on the arms of the chair. He begins
very slightly to shake. Immediately, George, standing behind him, reaches
his right hand down on his shoulder with a firm pressure. Anthony puts his
own hand up and covers it for a moment. Then he braces himself upright,
takes his hat and cane and gives them to George with a whispered word.
George puts them on the little table and returns to his place behind the
chair*

*Father Barrett hurries in R. He nods to Matron and Sister, crosses and
shakes hands with Anthony, then stands on the right-hand side of the
altar*

The music starts again—very softly. George glances at his watch

George This is it, sir. Up to the firing line—and all the luck in the world.
(*He moves Anthony's chair across R and turns it to face the altar. He
stands on Anthony's right*)

*The music pauses and commences again, softly playing the Lohengrin
Bridal March. Sister Winifred, Matron, Nurse Rowlands and Polly stand up*

*With the background of music, the little procession enters R. Chrissy on
Sir's right arm, followed by Annie. Chrissy does not wear a bridal gown,
but a pretty long silk dress and a wide brimmed hat trimmed with
flowers. She carries a little Victorian nosegay. Sir is magnificent in
formal morning dress, carrying a silk hat in his left hand. Annie is
almost unrecognizable in a well cut summer suit and wearing a large
hat trimmed with feathers. She carries a large bouquet*

*They reach the altar. Sir leads Chrissy to stand on Anthony's left. Annie
moves back a little so that Sir may move to stand on the right of the altar
below Father Barrett. Chrissy and Anthony look at each other. He holds
out his hand. She turns and gives her flowers to Annie, then moves back
and takes Anthony's hand for a moment. Then, finally, she turns to face the
altar*

*The music comes to its triumphant last chord and the Vicar opens his book.
There is a fraction of silence before he speaks*

Vicar Dearly beloved, we are gathered together in the sight of God...

*The curtain is lowered for a few moments to denote the passing of eight
hours*

The scene is unchanged—except for a coffee tray on the little table L. *The
altar is still lit. Anthony's cap and stick have been removed*

*Sister Winifred, Father Barrett and Brother Francis have drawn up three
chairs before the altar and are relaxing over a cup of coffee*

Francis Well, no-one can possibly say this has not been a perfect day.
Winifred Absolutely. I hope Anthony wasn't exhausted.
Barrett He was splendid. And what a speech—he really is a most able
young man.
Winifred I can only hope it will turn out well. They are both devoted—
and intelligent.
Francis No-one could possibly have done more for them. (*To Father
Barrett*) I am so glad, so very glad you were able to be here, sir. How
long have you been at St Leo's?
Barrett Over twenty years. I was not much older than you are when I first
came.

*Sister Winifred gets up and takes Father Barrett's cup to the table for a
refill*

Francis You will no doubt miss it when you leave.

*A pause. A spoon clatters on the coffee tray. Sister Winifred does not turn.
During the following conversation, she stands with her back to the two
men*

I saw the notice of your posting in the Gazette. Africa—have you always been interested in the missionary field?

Barrett I felt I would like to experience it before I'm too old.

Francis Yes, indeed. But—Africa?

Barrett Tanzania, actually. I heard there was a vacancy at the St Cuthbert's Mission Hospital at Mukinge*. Fortunately, they insisted on someone with hospital experience, so I got the posting.

Francis When do you leave?

There is a very slight pause

Barrett At the end of the week.

Sister Winifred brings Father Barrett his coffee cup and gives it to him without speaking or looking at him. She returns to the tray and stands with her back to them. The soft church chime sounds the half hour

Francis Good Heavens—(*he glances at his wrist-watch*) I must take my leave. (*He gets up and crosses to put his cup on the tray*)

Sister Winifred takes his hat down from the peg and gives it to him

His Lordship will want to know every detail of this day—and how I shall enjoy giving it to him. (*He holds out his hand*) Goodbye, Sister Winifred. I do hope we meet again. And if ever Castleside may help St Leo's—in any way—promise me you will ask.

Winifred (*taking his hand*) I will indeed. And God bless you for the help which made this day possible.

Francis No—yours was the initial inspiration. And we must wish those two young people well and remember them in our prayers. (*He shakes her hand warmly and turns to Father Barrett*)

Father Barrett puts his cup on the altar

Goodbye, Father Barrett. I have been privileged to meet you. And I hope you will find great joy and fulfilment in your new life.

Barrett Thank you. The final analysis must, of course, be in the hands of God.

---

*Pronounced "Mew-kinge"

Francis Always.

The two men shake hands warmly. Sister Winifred takes the cup from the altar to the tray, turns and moves to the window, with her back to the room

Brother Francis goes out R

Father Barrett shuts the door and stands with his back to it

Barrett How could I possibly have foreseen you would hear in such a fashion?

Winifred (*turning and coming* C *to face him*) Why have you not spoken to me before?

Barrett I could never have done so before the wedding. And in any case I had to find the right moment. In this busy place you are not often alone.

Winifred I am alone now.

He looks at her but does not answer. She breaks the pause

And I do not understand. This news will be devastating for St Leo's. The whole place should be buzzing like a beehive. And all is silent. Why?

Barrett Because you are the first to know.

Winifred How can that be?

Barrett It has become an emergency. I was not due to leave for another three months.

Winifred But...

Barrett I was to replace an ailing man. He died very suddenly and unexpectedly—last week. I have had to make hurried arrangements. I shall tell Matron—officially—this evening. Tomorrow it will be public knowledge. At this moment you are—as I have always intended—the first to know.

Winifred But, Father—why?

He does not answer

(*More insistently*) Why?

Barrett Do you not know? (*He comes* C *to face her*)

Winifred (*slowly*) It seems—I need you to tell me.

Barrett Because... (*He pauses again, then speaks with some difficulty*)

It is—sometimes—expedient—to put a space—between certain eventualities.

Winifred A warm working friendship. Over twenty years. Could you not have continued to trust me after so long?

Barrett Implicitly. But you are the stronger, Winifred, you always have been.

Winifred So?

Barrett I have to consider whether—I can no longer trust myself.

Winifred But—twenty years…

Barrett (*suddenly*) Tell me, in all that time—has there never been a moment—a brief second—when you have not seen that friendship as … as something more?

Winifred (*suddenly anguished*) Do not ask me that! You must not make me answer that! (*She turns up past him to the altar and leans against it*)

Barrett (*quickly*) No—I must not. Forgive me, I was wrong.

Winifred Do you intend—later perhaps—to come back?

Barrett I do not think that will be advisable.

Winifred I shall—miss you.

Barrett I, too.

Winifred Do we—write?

Barrett Occasionally—perhaps. But not at great length. Remember, we both have our final and most sacred commitment.

Winifred Yes. (*Slowly*) When do you finally—leave?

Barrett On Friday morning. I will ask that there be no official farewell, or send off. I shall pack in the morning and go to London—as I have often done. In the evening I shall not come back to the peace of St Leo's—but be on a plane to darkest Africa.

Winifred Where you will bring much light.

Barrett Thank you.

Winifred I would like to say—you did realize how much—this little wedding meant to me.

Barrett Yes.

Winifred Then you will understand how deeply I thank you—and shall remember you for the generous—and caring motivation—which made it possible.

Barrett At least I may leave you with that.

Winifred Always.

There is a pause

Do we say goodbye—here and now?
Barrett Yes.

She straightens up, then crosses to meet him C

Winifred (*steadily*) Goodbye, old friend. And God go with you. (*She holds out her hand*)

He slowly takes it

Barrett Sister Winifred, (*he pauses*) may God bless and be with The Wayward Spirit every hour of every day—until he finally receives it into the eternal glory of His everlasting arms. (*He looks at her for a moment, then releases her hand and goes to the door* R)

She abruptly turns her back. He pauses with his hand on the door handle, then turns back and goes to her. He gently puts a hand on her arm, and turns her to face him. They look at each other. Then he reaches out his right arm, and with his thumb marks her forehead with the sign of the cross

Then he turns and goes out quickly R, *shutting the door behind him*

Sister Winifred stands very still for a moment. Suddenly she turns, and looks up into the left-hand corner of the room

Winifred Oh. How could you! How could you give so much with one hand—and take away so much more with the other? (*She stands still for a moment, then goes to the altar and stands resting her right hand on it, her left hand covering her eyes. Then she pulls a handkerchief from her pocket. Father Barrett's letter falls out. She opens and reads it. Then, without showing any emotion, she replaces it in the envelope and returns it to her pocket*)

The phone rings. She ignores it. It continues to ring. Suddenly, she straightens up, wipes her eyes, pockets the handkerchief, and goes slowly to pick up the receiver

(*Desperately*) Oh, Olive dear—not now... (*She pauses, suddenly alert*) Sister Carr—yes. ... When? ... How many? ... Where are we putting them? ... Number five. Good. Has Dr O'Connell been...? There already. Yes, at once. ... You need—yes—yes—and Coromine. I'll collect it all on my way over. ... Yes—I have the keys. (*She puts down the phone and hurries to the altar. She lifts up the front drapery and opens the middle drawer of the desk and takes out a bunch of keys. She closes the drawer and replaces the drapery. She puts the keys in her pocket—then runs off* L, *returning almost at once, struggling into her stiff white apron*)

She moves C, *then pauses and looks up to the left corner*

Later!

She runs out R, *leaving the door open behind her*

The loud clangour of an approaching ambulance suddenly fills the quiet room, comes nearer, and stops

The CURTAIN *falls gently on the lighted altar—symbol of everlasting faith and hope*

PRODUCTION NOTE

This play has a large cast and takes place in a busy hospital where there are few, if any, static moments. Therefore, the script contains detailed movements, and if any companies are willing to at least try these movements, it should be found that everyone should be in the right place at the right time to do—and say—the right thing.

Hospital procedures

There are several incidents in Act I which are necessary to show at once Anthony's semi-helpless state. George's tray on the little table should be carefully set with a small enamel bowl, the razor, its case, two small hand towels (the size of face cloths), and a tin of talcum powder. The back massage may be tricky if Anthony is ticklish—or coy! So, George first turns the chair C, facing the audience. He then gently helps Anthony to lean well forward—fitting in his dialogue as he goes. Then he puts talcum powder on his hands, stands on Anthony's left, lifts the shirt slightly with his left hand, and with his right hand makes gentle rubbing motions, using the lifted shirt as a screen. Then he wipes off his hands on one of the small towels, returns it to the tray and then gently helps Anthony back to a sitting position. NOTE: the talcum tin should be empty. Spillage might be a bad hold-up!

During Sister Winifred's narrative about St Leo's foundation, George is cleaning the razor. He should not flap the towel as the movement may detract from her speaking. Nurse Rowlands should by now have folded her laundry ready in the bag, but may retain one item—say a towel—draped over her arm as she listens. At the end, she folds that last item and puts it in the bag, timing this just as Polly enters to collect it.

The amount of laundry needed should be worked out between the actress playing Nurse Rowlands and the producer: perhaps two sheets, two pillowcases, two towels—even a pair of pyjamas. Rehearsals will tell.

In Act I, when Sister Winifred gives Anthony his injection, she should hold the syringe up in front of her just above eye level, pull the plunger gently down about an inch, then raise it again, place her hand beside his extended arm on the chair and mime pressing the plunger.

Lifting Anthony back into his chair may need to be carefully rehearsed. It is a piece of trained nursing skill and should not be clumsy. The secret is to have their arms firmly under his armpits, and on the word "Lift" act smoothly and together.

Anthony's "Ouch" is simply the spoken word in his ordinary voice. He does not wince or whine. (After all, he has been in the Army!)

Father Barrett must sit down beside Anthony at the end of Act I. He should not loom over him—in his sombre black cassock—when he is being soothing and sympathetic.

If in the scene between Anthony and Sir (Act I) neither men are smokers, the cigarette business may be cut—but this would be a pity. Sir deliberately starts his visit by making a joke about Nurse Potter, which gets Anthony laughing. Then they both relax over a cigarette—and Sir begins slowly and gently to work up to the moment when he can no longer withold the tragic news.

Sister Winifred has an enormous part in Act II where she is taking on the Catholic hierarchy by telephone—the scene is practically a monologue. But, she has a large writing pad in front of her, on which she makes notes—and doodles. Her dialogue may be written clearly on this pad—she can read off as she writes.

In the last scene, with Father Barrett, Sister Winifred only seems as if she will break for one moment—("You must not make me answer that!") then she controls herself. The last moments of this scene must be played with the two of them dead stage centre. And hold the pause when he comes back and turns her to face him. The audience will be expecting a last embrace. Instead, they get the sign of the cross.

The movements on Page 61 are particularly important. When Chrissy pushes Anthony's chair LC and turns it to face R, she has not only got him correctly facing Brother Francis, but the chair is already positioned facing the door R for a neat and uncluttered exit when they all finally go to lunch.

Charlotte Hastings

FURNITURE AND PROPERTY LIST

ACT I

Scene 1

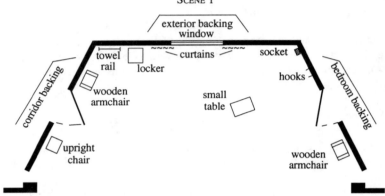

On stage: Floor length, dark crimson curtains

Large hospital locker. *On it:* ashtray; tray containing bottles, glasses, enamel hospital bowl, folded towels

Towel rail

Pile of linen, sheets, towels, and pillow cases

2 small wooden armchairs

Plain wooden upright chair

Man's long warm dressing gown

Anthony's light khaki cardigan jacket

Light motorised wheelchair

Small sliding bedside-type table. *On it:* tray containing small bowl, razor case, two towels, tin of talcum powder, regimental tie

Razor

Off stage: Large enamel bowl covered with a white towel (**Nurse Rowlands**)

Large black plastic sack labelled "St Leo's Laundry" in white (**Nurse Rowlands**)

Small kidney bowl. *In it:* ready charged hypodermic syringe, cotton swabs (**Sister Winifred**)

Full laundry bag (**Polly**)

Small flask containing liquid (**Father Barrett**)

2 filled carrier bags—one with a bottle showing, large bunch of flowers (**Chrissy**)

Personal: **Sir:** stethoscope, cigarette case containing cigarettes, lighter, wrist-watch (worn throughout), mobile phone

Sister Winifred: wrist-watch (worn throughout)

Father Barrett: wrist-watch (worn throughout)

George: wrist-watch (worn throughout)

SCENE 2

On stage: As before

Set: Little table R above door

Small armchair RC for **Chrissy**

Off stage: Folded newspaper, envelopes (**Father Barrett**)

Personal: **Sister Winifred:** handkerchief

ACT II

SCENE 1

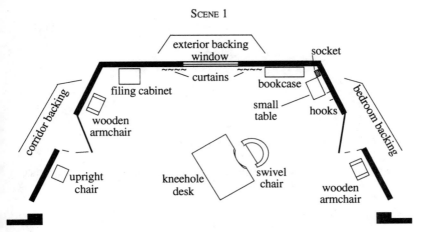

On stage: Floor length, dark crimson curtains

Tall modern metal filing cabinet. *On it:* stacked files and papers

Small wooden table. *On it:* filing basket full of papers, containing, at the very bottom, a large glossy folder—dark blue with a gold crown on it

Large crucifix

2 small armchairs

Small upright chair

Large framed reproduction of The Last Supper

Wooden bookcase crammed with books (more neatly arranged), including a large book—*Glasswell's*

Big oak kneehole desk, its drawers containing large envelope, large writing pad, file, bunch of keys. *On it:* files, papers, telephone, pen

Large comfortable swivel chair

Off stage: Books, papers (**Sister Winifred**)
Large pile of files in assorted covers (**Polly**)
Large piece of printed paper (**Annie**)

Scene 2

On stage: As before

Check: Swivel chair behind desk, upright chair opposite, armchair end of desk facing audience

Off stage: Pile of papers (**Sister Winifred**)
Fair-sized parcel wrapped in fancy paper with a card on top (**Polly**)

ACT III

Scene 1

On stage: As before

Check: **Sister Winifred**'s apron on hook

Off stage: Silver tray. *On it:* silver coffee pot, cream jug, cups and saucers, plate of biscuits (**Polly**)

Personal: **George:** file of papers
Brother Francis: wide brimmed black hat, handkerchief, wrist-watch (worn throughout)

SCENE 2

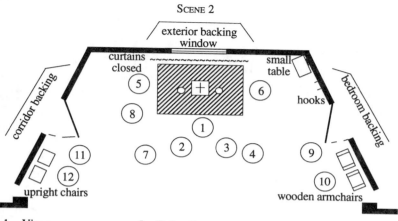

1	Vicar	5	Father Barrett	9	Nurse Rowlands
2	Chrissy	6	Brother Francis	10	Polly
3	Anthony	7	Annie	11	Matron
4	George	8	Sir	12	Sister Winifred

Set: Red curtains drawn
          Desk DC, phone on floor beside it
          George's dark jacket
          Brother Francis' long black cassock and black hat

Strike: **Sister Winifred's** apron from hook L

Off stage: Small upright chair (**Brother Francis**)
          Large square cardboard box neatly covered with purple cloth (**Helper**)
          Folded purple cloth (**George**)
          Handsome brass cross, about three feet high (**Helpers**)
          2 silver vases containing roses (**Sister Winifred**)
          Braided cap, small swagger stick (**Anthony**)

Personal: **George:** 3 envelopes, 2 containing telegrams
          Nurse Rowlands: piece of pasteboard, handkerchief
          Polly: piece of pasteboard
          Vicar: large prayer book
          Chrissy: little Victorian nosegay
          Annie: large bouquet

During the Curtain fall on page 80
Strike: **Anthony's** cap and stick
Set: Coffee tray with cups and saucers, spoons, etc. on table L
          Brother Francis' hat on peg L

LIGHTING PLOT

Property fittings required: nil
2 interior locations

ACT I, Scene 1

To open: Bright summer morning lighting

No cues

ACT I, Scene 2

To open: Bright summer morning lighting

No cues

ACT II, Scene 1

To open: Overall general lighting

No cues

ACT II, Scene 2

To open: Summer morning lighting

No cues

ACT III, Scene 1

To open: Overall general lighting

No cues

ACT III, Scene 2

To open: Interior lighting (curtains drawn)

Cue 1   **George** reaches behind the curtains   (Page 72)
           Snap on soft golden light on the altar

EFFECTS PLOT

ACT I

---

* See next page

Cue 10 **The Vicar, George**, and **Anthony** chat together   (Page 79)
          Soft strain of music*

Cue 11 **Matron** opens the door   (Page 79)
          Music increases in volume*

Cue 12 **Sister Winifred** sits beside **Matron**   (Page 79)
          Cut music

Cue 13 **Father Barrett** stands on the right-hand side of the altar   (Page 79)
          Very soft music*

Cue 14 **George** stands on Anthony's right   (Page 79)
          *Music pauses and starts again, softly playing the Lohengrin Bridal
          March to its last chord**

Cue 15 **Sister Winifred** turns to the tray   (Page 81)
          Soft church chime sounds the half hour

Cue 16 **Sister Winifred** puts the letter in her pocket   (Page 84)
          Phone rings

Cue 17 **Sister Winifred** runs out ʀ   (Page 85)
          *Loud clangour of approaching ambulance, comes
          nearer, then stops*

---

* A tape recording of non-copyright music, played on an instrument similar to that mentioned
in this play, is available on loan from Samuel French Ltd